ALSO IN THIS SERIES

On Bearing Unbearable States of Mind Ruth Riesenberg-Malcolm. Edited by Priscilla Roth

Psychoanalysis on the Move: The Work of Joseph Sandler Edited by Peter Fonagy, Arnold M. Cooper and Robert S. Wallerstein

The Dead Mother: The Work of André Green Edited by Gregorio Kohon

The Fabric of Affect in the Psychoanalytic Discourse André Green

The Bi-Personal Field: Experiences of Child Analysis Antonino Ferro

The Dove that Returns, the Dove that Vanishes: Paradox and Creativity in Psychoanalysis Michael Parsons

Ordinary People, Extra-ordinary Protections: A Post-Kleinian Approach to the Treatment of Primitive Mental States Judith Mitrani

The Violence of Interpretation: From Pictogram to Statement Piera Aulagnier

The Importance of Fathers: A Psychoanalytic Re-Evaluation Judith Trowell and Alicia Etchegoyen

Dreams That Turn Over a Page: Paradoxical Dreams in Psychoanalysis Jean-Michel Quinodoz

The Couch and the Silver Screen: Psychoanalytic Reflections on European Cinema Edited and introduced by Andrea Sabbadini

In Pursuit of Psychic Change: The Betty Joseph Workshop Edited by Edith Hargreaves and Arturo Varchevker

The Quiet Revolution in American Psychoanalysis: Selected Papers of Arnold M. Cooper Arnold M. Cooper. Edited and introduced by Elizabeth L. Auchincloss

Seeds of Illness and Seeds of Recovery: The Genesis of Suffering and the Role of Psychoanalysis Antonino Ferro

The Work of Psychic Figurability: Mental States Without Representation César Botella and Sára Botella

Key Ideas for a Contemporary Psychoanalysis: Misrecognition and Recognition of the Unconscious André Green

The Telescoping of Generations: Listening to the Narcissistic Links Between Generations Haydée Faimberg

Glacial Times: A Journey Through the World of Madness Salomon Resnik

This Art of Psychoanalysis: Dreaming Undreamt Dreams and Interrupted Cries Thomas H. Ogden

Psychoanalysis as Therapy and Storytelling Antonino Ferro

Psychoanalysis and Religion in the 21st Century: Competitors or Collaborators? Edited by David M. Black

Recovery of the Lost Good Object Eric Brenman. Edited and introduced by Gigliola Fornari Spoto

The Many Voices of Psychoanalysis Roger Kennedy

Feeling the Words: Neuropsychoanalytic Understanding of Memory and the Unconscious Mauro Mancia

Projected Shadows: Psychoanalytic Reflections on the Representation of Loss in European Cinema Edited by Andrea Sabbadini

Encounters with Melanie Klein: Selected Papers of Elizabeth Spillius Elizabeth Spillius. Edited by Priscilla Roth and Richard Rusbridger

TITLES IN THE NEW LIBRARY OF PSYCHOANALYSIS TEACHING SERIES

Creative Readings
Essays on Seminal Analytic Works

Thomas H. Ogden

Routledge
Taylor & Francis Group
LONDON AND NEW YORK

First published 2012
by Routledge
27 Church Road, Hove, East Sussex BN3 2FA

Simultaneously published in the USA and Canada
by Routledge
711 Third Avenue, New York NY 10017

Routledge is an imprint of the Taylor & Francis Group, an Informa Business

British Library Cataloguing in Publication Data
A catalogue record for this book is available from the British Library

Library of Congress Cataloging in Publication Data
Ogden, Thomas H.
　Creative readings : essays on seminal analytic works / Thomas Ogden.
　　p. cm.—(New library of psychoanalysis)
　Includes bibliographical references and index.
　ISBN 978-0-415-69832-0 (hardback)—ISBN 978-0-415-69833-7 (paperback)
　1. Psychoanalysis.　I. Title.
　RC506.O33 2013
　616.8917—dc23

2011036755

ISBN: 978-0-415-69832-0 (hbk)
ISBN: 978-0-415-69833-7 (pbk)
ISBN: 978-0-203-12529-8 (ebk)

Typeset in Bembo
by RefineCatch Limited, Bungay, Suffolk
Paperback cover design by Sandra Heath

MIX
Paper from
responsible sources
FSC www.fsc.org FSC® C004839

Printed and bound in Great Britain by
TJ International Ltd, Padstow, Cornwall

To my patients who, each in their
own way, have taught me what is
possible when two people put their
all into talking truthfully to one another

Contents

Acknowledgements

I would like to thank the *International Journal of Psychoanalysis* for permission to use the following papers in this volume:

A new reading of the origins of object-relations theory. *International Journal of Psychoanalysis* 83: 767–782, 2002. Copyright The Institute of Psychoanalysis.

An introduction to the reading of Bion. *International Journal of Psychoanalysis* 85: 285–300, 2004. Copyright The Institute of Psychoanalysis.

Reading Loewald: Oedipus reconceived. *International Journal of Psychoanalysis* 87: 651–666, 2006. Copyright The Institute of Psychoanalysis.

Elements of analytic style: Bion's clinical seminars. *International Journal of Psychoanalysis*, 88: 1185–1200, 2007. Copyright The Institute of Psychoanalysis.

Reading Harold Searles. *International Journal of Psychoanalysis* 88: 353–369, 2007. Copyright The Institute of Psychoanalysis.

Why read Fairbairn? *International Journal of Psychoanalysis* 91: 101–118, 2010. Copyright The Institute of Psychoanalysis.

Reading Susan Isaacs: Toward a radically revised theory of thinking. *International Journal of Psychoanalysis* 92: 925–942, 2011. Copyright The Institute of Psychoanalysis.

The *Psychoanalytic Quarterly* has kindly granted permission to use the following article in this volume:

Reading Winnicott. *Psychoanalytic Quarterly* 70: 299–323, 2001. Copyright the *Psychoanalytic Quarterly*.

Acknowledgements

I would like to thank Marta Schneider Brody for her perceptive editorial comments on many of the chapters of this volume. I am also grateful to Gina Atkinson and Patricia Marra for the thoughtfulness of their contributions to the production phase of the book, and to Yoav Efrati for his two drawings ("Reading people," 2007) that appear on the front and back covers.

Some thoughts on how to read this book

This volume is the product of more than a decade of writing my experience of reading major works by Freud, Fairbairn, Isaacs, Winnicott, Loewald, Bion, and Searles. I attempt not *to write about* my experience of reading their works, but *to write my experience* of reading them: to write what I have let these papers and books do to me, what I have done with these papers and books, and how I have rewritten them and made them my own books and papers. I try to capture in my writing something of the way I read in order that the reader may learn something about the way he reads, including the way he reads his own writing. This volume is "a reading book" – a book about reading, about how to read – not simply a book of readings.

The experience of reading

When I am talking about a book that is important to me, I often slip and say, "the book I wrote," instead of, "the book I read," and then correct myself. I've heard others regularly make the same slip. I attribute the error to the fact that when we have spent a good deal of time with a book, we feel that we have written it or at least rewritten it – and, in an important sense, we have. Reading is an experience in which we do not simply "take in" the meaning of the text. In the act of reading, we transform the black markings on the page into linguistic structures that hold significance. But when we are reading creatively, we do something more than that. We each produce our own personal set of meanings and ideas using the text as a starting point: "Take the book into your two hands, and read your eyes out; you will never find what I find" (Emerson, 1841, p. 87). I think of this way of

1

reading – more accurately, this aspect of reading – as "transitive reading," a reading experience in which we are actively doing something to the text, making it our own, interpreting in a way that adds something to the text that had not been there before we have read it.

It is also important to be able to read "intransitively" – that is, to be able to give oneself over to the experience of reading. When reading, I try to allow myself to be occupied and, to a certain extent, taken over by the mind of another person, the writer, as I speak his or her words. When I read an analytic text, for instance a work of Melanie Klein, I "become a Kleinian" and view the world through her eyes. In teaching Klein's work, I ask students and colleagues to try on for size her ideas in their entirety as they read her work, and to do their best not to disrupt this experience of reading with such (knee jerk) objections as, "It is impossible for a two-day-old infant to fantasize in the way she is describing."

Giving oneself over to the experience of reading is by no means a detached or passive event. One is not only allowing "foreigners" (words and sentences that are not one's own) into oneself, one is also permitting oneself to be read by that foreigner (the writing). Of course, the writing cannot read us, but it can present us with a perspective on ourselves from which we have never viewed ourselves, and may never again be able *not* to include in the ways we view ourselves. The experience of "being read by the writing" (making use of the writing to engage in a form of self-reflection that is unique to the experience of reading) need not feel invasive or intrusive. On the contrary, in being read well by what one is reading (in using the experience of reading to read oneself), the reader may feel that he is becoming alive to a way of being that he has always felt to comprise an essential aspect of himself or herself, but has not known how to put into words, or how to more fully become the person who thinks and expresses himself in that way.

Winnicott's writing is remarkable in its power to read the reader (see Chapter 5). Take, for example, a sentence from "Primitive emotional development":

> It seems to me that there is in it [the baby's injuring his fingers or mouth by too vigorously sucking his thumb or hand] the element that something must suffer if the infant is to have pleasure: the object of primitive love suffers by being loved, apart from being hated.
>
> (Winnicott, 1945, p. 155)

2

In reading this sentence, there is sadness and beauty to the language, particularly in the words "the object of primitive love suffers by being loved." I have experienced the forcefulness, and even violence, of my children's primitive love and their primitive need for me when they were infants – and even now that they are well into adulthood. I, like most parents, have experienced sleep deprivation, agonizing worry and emotional fraying as a consequence of trying to meet their primitive love with love of my own. But, as Winnicott is saying in this sentence (in an accepting, but unsentimental voice), that is the nature of the beast – the nature of being the *object* of primitive love.

Winnicott uses the word *object* in this sentence not in its usual technical sense (i.e. as a synonym for a person in the external object world or a figure in the internal object world), but in its everyday sense (the object of the transitive verb *love*: the person on whom, toward whom, against whom primitive love is directed). I, like most parents, would not trade a moment of being the object of that kind of love. More difficult for me to fully and genuinely acknowledge in reading and being read by Winnicott are the ways in which my own primitive love, both as a child and as an adult, has caused others – particularly my parents, my wife, and my children – to suffer. And that, too, is inescapably the nature of the beast.

Reading as interpreting: Adding something new

With the exception of Isaacs, all of the analysts whose work I discuss were prolific writers. I have chosen to look closely at one or two pieces of the writing of each author. I have selected these partic-ular articles and books because my experience of reading and rereading them, and of metaphorically writing and rewriting them, has played a singularly important role in my development as a psychoanalyst. I try to stay true to each of the texts in the sense of accurately conveying (in part by citing the texts at some length) the author's ideas and the way he or she expresses them. My emphasis, however, is not on trying to determine what Freud or Bion or Isaacs or Loewald "really meant." I am far more interested in what these authors knew, but did not know they knew – in how these texts are rich in ways their authors did not consciously intend or understand.

3

My reading (and writing) in this way will inevitably lead the reader to ask where the author's thinking leaves off and where mine begins. For example, when I say in Chapter 3 that it is "implicit" in Isaacs' (1952) "The nature and function of phantasy" that inherent to phantasy is the need to discover, to get to know and understand external reality, I mean that, *for me*, the language Isaacs uses strongly suggests that idea. Did she have that in mind (consciously) when she wrote the paper? Probably not, but I believe that the language she uses suggests that her thinking was leading in that direction. I support that idea by looking at her use of language in the final portion of her paper where she states that the symbolic function of phantasy "builds a bridge from the inner world to interest in the outer world and knowledge of physical objects and events" (Isaacs, 1952, p. 110). She goes on to say that phantasying promotes "the development of interest in the external world and the process of learning about it" (p. 110). And a bit later: "The power to seek out and organize knowledge [of the external world] is drawn [from phantasy activity]" (p. 110). It is from these statements and others that I cite in my discussion of her paper that I make my inferences about the way in which the need to know gives direction to phantasy activity (which I view as synonymous with unconscious thinking).

One might ask how you, the reader, are to decide to whom to give credit or responsibility for the inferences I draw/create. A part of my response to that question is: Who cares? The important thing is what one is able to do with the ideas that Isaacs makes explicit in combination with the ideas that her language suggests. In my reading of Isaacs I may be able to do more with aspects of the text than Isaacs was able to because I – as is the case for every contemporary analytic reader – have available to me perspectives derived from developments in psychoanalysis and related fields that Isaacs did not. To my ear, her text echoes work published decades after she wrote her paper, for example, Chomsky's (1957, 1968) work on the deep structure of language, Bion's (1962a, 1962b) work on a psychoanalytic theory of thinking, and Winnicott's (1974) conception of "the fear of breakdown." In addition, and probably more important, I have a mind of my own that is different from Isaacs' mind, and that allows me to see in her work a good deal that she did not see. The same is true for you, the reader, in reading Isaacs and in reading what I write.

In the chapters that follow, I, at times, indicate that a particular idea is my own "extension" of an author's work, but in truth, I cannot say exactly where the author's thinking stops and mine begins. Ideas do not come with tags naming their owner.[1] For example, in my discussion of Fairbairn's work (Chapter 4, p. 62), I say

> It seems to me that a libidinal tie to an internal object toward whom one feels anger, resentment, and the like, necessarily involves an (unconscious) wish/need to use what control one feels one has to change the unloving and unaccepting (internal) object into a loving and accepting one.
>
> From this vantage point, I view the libidinal ego and the internal saboteur as aspects of self that are intent on transforming the exciting object and the rejecting object into loving objects.

In this passage, I am extending Fairbairn's thinking about internal object relations by stating that within the terms of the internal object world that Fairbairn describes, it seems to me that the most important motivating force driving the creation and maintenance of the unconscious internal object world is the need to transform unsatisfactory objects into satisfactory ones. Fairbairn, himself, never comes to this conclusion. You, the reader, will have to judge for yourself whether my extensions of Fairbairn's ideas are, indeed, consistent with Fairbairn's thinking, and whether they enrich or detract from his contribution. But I realize as I listen to my own words – "You, the reader, will have to judge for yourself whether my extensions of Fairbairn are, indeed, consistent with Fairbairn's thinking" – that this idea constitutes for me only a partial truth. To that perspective must be added another equally valid point of view: you, the reader, should feel no obligation to try to determine what is my thinking and what is Fairbairn's. In fact, the effort to do so is beside the point. What *is* important is what you *do* with Fairbairn's writing and with mine – what you *make* that is neither his nor mine, but your own.

Even if one were inclined to try to determine what is Fairbairn's and what is mine, the task, it seems to me, is impossible. Breuer, in

---

1 Just as ideas come without tags indicating who owns them, it is important that thinkers not come with tags indicating who owns them (for example, the tags "contemporary Kleinian," "contemporary Freudian," "self-psychologist," "relational analyst," and so on).

his introduction to the theoretical section of *Studies on Hysteria* (Breuer and Freud, 1893–1895), eloquently comments on the problems involved in claims of originality:

> When a science is making rapid advances, thoughts which were first expressed by single individuals quickly become common property. . . . It is scarcely possible to be certain who first gave them utterance, and there is always a danger of regarding as a product of one's own what has already been said by someone else. I hope, therefore, that I may be excused . . . if no strict distinction is made between what is my own and what originates elsewhere.
>
> (Breuer and Freud, 1893–1895, pp. 185–186)

Borges, in the preface to his first volume of poetry, *Fervor to Buenos Aires*, adds irony and wit, and an additional layer of complexity, to the idea that no one has the right to claim a poem (or an idea) as his own:

> If in the following pages there is some successful verse or other, may the reader forgive me the audacity of having written it before him. We are all one; our inconsequential minds are much alike, and circumstances so influence us that it is something of an accident that you are the reader and I the writer – the unsure, ardent writer – of my verses.
>
> (Borges, 1923, p. 269)

The irony here is that Borges, in a style of writing and thinking that is unmistakably original to him, is dismissing the idea that anyone is justified in claiming that his writing and thinking are strictly his own. The idea that the author cannot claim originality for his writing is not original to Borges, but Borges' way of expressing that idea – and at the same time refuting it – radically alters it, and makes it original to him.

What one says and the way one says it

Whether or not we believe that anyone has the right to attach his or her name to an idea or a poem or an essay or a particular form of "word music" (Borges, quoted by Vargas Llosa, 2008, p. 32), human truths must again and again be rediscovered in new forms, otherwise those truths become clichés that staunch the flow of genuine thinking and creativity. Renewal of thinking and originality of expression are mutually dependent: writing is a unique form of thinking; and originality of writing *is* originality of thinking. Neither content nor style exists without the other. Nevertheless, if, for a moment, we think of content as the anatomy of writing, then style is its physiology. Content, in the absence of style, is a lifeless corpse; style, without content, is an insubstantial wraith. Together, style and content comprise the living, working body of writing waiting to be read. It is for this reason that in discussing the books and papers that are the subject of each of the chapters of this volume, I treat writing style and ideational content as two qualities of a single entity – one cannot say the same thing in two different ways: to say something differently is to say something different.

For example, in reading the following sentence from Freud's (1917a) "Mourning and melancholia" (see Chapter 2), it is impossible to separate the ideas from the writing:

> Just as mourning impels the ego to give up the object by declaring the object to be dead and offering the ego the inducement of continuing to live, so does each single struggle of ambivalence [in melancholia] loosen the fixation of the libido to the object by disparaging it, denigrating it and even as it were killing it.
>
> (p. 257)

The writing is dense – a great deal of thinking is occurring in the very act of writing a few words. It could be argued that the entirety of the central argument of this watershed paper is present either implicitly or explicitly in this single sentence. In comparing the mental activities that lie at the heart of mourning with those operating in melancholia, Freud not only describes but also captures in the action of the language what he has in mind. Freud's belief that the aim both of mourning and of melancholia is the same – to cope with the loss of a person to whom one is deeply attached – is not stated as such, but is present in the structure of the sentence: "Just as . . . so does."

He uses animism in this sentence – a literary device that is a hallmark of his writing – to create an imaginary scene in which mourning is an active agent with a life of its own that does something critical to the self (the ego): "mourning impels the ego to give up the object by

7

declaring the object to be dead." Mourning does so by "offering the ego the inducement of continuing to live." This is quite a statement (contained in a single clause): entering the process of mourning involves an unconscious choice to continue to be emotionally alive in a world marred by the absence of the person one loves. The experience of mourning is in itself a form of "continuing to live" – mourning *is* living in a world devoid of the person one loves. Not to mourn is to allow an aspect of oneself to die emotionally in order to avoid the pain of living without the person one loves.

In the second half of this sentence, Freud begins by naming the essential similarity and the essential difference between the mourner and the melancholic: "so does [the melancholic in] each single struggle of ambivalence loosen the fixation of the libido to the object." In other words, the melancholic, like the mourner, is faced by the prospect of experiencing the pain of attachment to an absent object. Also like the mourner, the melancholic, in "each single struggle of ambivalence" – a phrase that captures the anguish experienced by the melancholic as he wrestles with himself – tries (in vain) to "loosen" his tie to the object.

The difference between the mourner and the melancholic lies in the fact that the melancholic is unable to face a life devoid of the lost person on whom his libido is "fixated"; consequently, he unconsciously opts not for life ("continuing to live"), but for a substitute for living in the form of the satisfaction entailed in unceasing rage at the absent loved object. This feeling state sustains the illusion (the unconscious psychic reality) that the absent person is still alive and capable of perceiving and feeling the melancholic's agony and his sense of having been profoundly wronged. The melancholic never tires of "disparaging, denigrating and even as it were killing it" (the lost, but psychically present object). What a masterful final phrase: "even as it were killing it." The melancholic does not kill the object, he only "as it were" kills it – the melancholic has it both ways: he kills the object (and in so doing, psychically takes control of a situation in which he feels powerless), *and* he does not "really" kill it (even in his own mind, especially in his own mind) because he needs to keep the object alive psychically so that it may witness his ceaseless raging at it and disparaging of it.

Part of what is distinctive to Freud in this remarkable sentence is the way in which the writing is alive with daring, but not reckless, conjecture compacted into a very few carefully chosen words, phrases and clauses. The writing has the quality of a tightly wound spring: it is subtly explosive.

8

To study Freud's writing is to study his thinking, and to study his thinking is to study his writing. The same is true – each in its own way – of all of the other authors whose work I discuss in this volume. In each of the sentences that follow there is an original way of thinking that is inseparable from a distinctive way of writing.

Who but Isaacs could have captured in a single sentence the ubiquity of phantasy in unconscious psychological life:

All impulses, all feelings, all modes of defence are experienced in phantasies which give them *mental* life and show their direction and purpose.

(Isaacs, 1952, p. 99)

Who but Fairbairn could have named and responded to the core of Isaacs' thinking in such cogent, diametrically opposing terms as these:

I cannot refrain from voicing the opinion that the explanatory concept of 'phantasy' has been rendered obsolete by the concepts of 'psychical reality' and 'internal objects' . . . These internal objects should be regarded as having an organized structure, an identity of their own, an endopsychic existence, and an activity as real within the inner world as those of any objects in the outer world.

(Fairbairn, 1943a, p. 359)

Who but Winnicott could have refused to adopt either Isaacs' or Fairbairn's or anybody else's language and ideas, and developed an altogether different form of writing and thinking that can be clearly heard in the following sentences:

An example of unintegration phenomena is provided by the very common experience of the patient who proceeds to give every detail of the week-end and feels contented at the end if everything has been said, though the analyst feels that no analytic work has been done . . . To be known means to feel integrated at least in the person of the analyst. This is the ordinary stuff of infant life, and an infant who has had no one person to gather his bits together starts with a handicap in his own self-integrating task . . . There are long stretches of time in a normal infant's life in which a baby does not mind whether he is many bits or one whole being, or whether he lives in his mother's face or in his own body, provided that from time to time he comes together and feels something.

(Winnicott, 1945, p. 150)

Who but Searles could have invented a style of writing that is as shockingly honest as the analytic experience itself:

while we [he and his hospitalized schizophrenic patient] were sitting in silence and a radio not far away was playing a tenderly romantic song . . . I realized that this man was dearer to me than anyone else in the world, including my wife.

(Searles, 1959, p. 294)

Who but Bion could have introduced a set of revolutionary analytic ideas in sentences as simple and enigmatic as these:

the patient who cannot dream cannot go to sleep and cannot wake up. Hence the peculiar condition seen clinically when a psychotic patient behaves as if he were in precisely this state.

(Bion, 1962a, p. 8)

And, who but Loewald could have written a sentence as profound and disturbing and so patently true as this one:

If we do not shrink from blunt language, in our role as children of our parents, by genuine emancipation we do kill something vital in them – not all in one blow and not in all respects, but contributing to their dying.

(Loewald, 1979, p. 395)

Perhaps the most important measure of the worth of this volume is the degree to which I am able to find in the texts I discuss more than what was there before I read them. While the words on the page remain the same, what changes when I am successful in reading creatively are the meanings of the words and sentences, meanings that have been waiting to be found, but have never until the present moment found a reader to discover them, to be changed by them, and to change those potential meanings in the process of discovering them.

Freud's "Mourning and melancholia" and the origins of object relations theory

Some writers write what they think; others think what they write. The latter seem to do their thinking in the very act of writing, as if thoughts arise from the conjunction of pen and paper, the work unfolding by surprise as it goes. Freud in many of his most important books and articles, including "Mourning and melancholia" (1917a), was a writer of this latter sort. In these writings, Freud made no attempt to cover his tracks, for example, his false starts, his uncertainties, his reversals of thinking (often done mid-sentence), his shelving of compelling ideas for the time being because they seemed to him too speculative or lacking adequate clinical foundation.

The legacy that Freud left was not simply a set of ideas, but, as important, and inseparable from those ideas, a new way of thinking about human experience that gave rise to nothing less than a new form of human subjectivity. Each of his psychoanalytic writings, from this point of view, is simultaneously an explication of a set of concepts and a demonstration of a newly created way of thinking about and experiencing ourselves.

I have chosen to look closely at Freud's "Mourning and melancholia" for two reasons. First, I consider this paper to be one of Freud's most important contributions in that it develops for the first time, in a systematic way, a line of thought which later would be termed "object relations theory" (Fairbairn, 1952). I use the term object relations theory to refer to a group of psychoanalytic theories holding in common a loosely knit set of metaphors that address the intrapsychic and interpersonal effects of relationships among unconscious "internal" objects, that is, among unconscious split-off parts of the personality. This line of thought has played a major role in shaping psychoanalysis from 1917 onward. Second, I have found that attending closely to Freud's writing as writing in "Mourning and melancholia" provides an extraordinary opportunity not only to listen to Freud think, but also, through the writing, to enter into that thinking process with him. In this way, the reader may learn a good deal about what is distinctive to the new form of thinking (and its attendant subjectivity) that Freud was in the process of creating in this article.

Freud wrote "Mourning and melancholia" in less than three months in early 1915 during a period that was for him filled with great intellectual and emotional upheaval. Europe was in the throes of the First World War. Despite his protestations, two of Freud's sons volunteered for military service and fought on the front lines. Freud was at the same time in the grips of intense intellectual foment. In the years 1914 and 1915, he wrote a series of 12 essays which represented his first major revision of psychoanalytic theory since the publication of *The Interpretation of Dreams* (1900). Freud's intent was to publish these papers as a book to be titled "Preliminaries to a metapsychology." He hoped that this collection would "provide a stable theoretical foundation for psycho-analysis" (Freud, quoted by Strachey, 1957, p. 105).

In the summer of 1915, Freud wrote to Ferenczi, "The twelve articles are, as it were, ready" (Gay, 1988, p. 367). As the phrase "as it were" suggests, Freud had misgivings about what he had written. Only five of the essays – all of which are groundbreaking papers – were ever published: "Instincts and their vicissitudes" (1915a), "Repression" (1915b), and "The unconscious" (1915c) were published as journal articles in 1915. "A metapsychological supplement to the theory of dreams" and "Mourning and melancholia," although completed in 1915, were not published until 1917. Freud destroyed the other seven articles which, he told Ferenczi, "deserved suppression and silence" (Gay, 1988, p. 373). None of these articles were shown to even his innermost circle of friends. Freud's reasons for "silencing" these essays remain a mystery in the history of psychoanalysis.

In the discussion that follows, I take up five portions of the text of "Mourning and melancholia," each of which contains a pivotal contribution to the analytic understanding of the unconscious work of mourning and of melancholia; at the same time, I look at the way

Freud made use of this seemingly focal exploration of these two psychological states as a vehicle for introducing – as much implicitly as explicitly – the foundations of his theory of unconscious internal object relations. (I am using Strachey's 1957 translation of "Mourning and melancholia" [1917a] in the *Standard Edition of the Complete Psychological Works of Sigmund Freud* as the text for my discussion. It is beyond the scope of this paper to address questions relating to the quality of that translation.)

The disturbance of self-regard

Freud's unique voice resounds in the opening sentence of "Mourning and melancholia":

> Dreams having served us as the prototype in normal life of narcissistic mental disorders, we will now try to throw some light on the nature of melancholia by comparing it with the normal affect of mourning.
>
> (p. 243)

The voice we hear in Freud's writing is remarkably constant through the 23 volumes of the *Standard Edition*. It is a voice with which no other psychoanalyst has written because no other analyst has had the right do so. The voice Freud creates is that of the founding father of a new discipline. Less than a year before writing "Mourning and melancholia," Freud (1914a) remarked that no one need wonder about his role in the history of psychoanalysis: "Psycho-analysis is my creation; for ten years I was the only person who concerned himself with it" (p. 7). Already in the opening sentence of this paper, something quite remarkable can be heard which we regularly take for granted in reading Freud: in the course of the 20 years preceding the writing of this sentence, Freud had not only created a revolutionary conceptual system, he had altered language itself. It is for me astounding to observe that virtually every word in the opening sentence has acquired in Freud's hands new meanings and a new set of relationships, not only to practically every other word in the sentence, but to innumerable words in language as a whole. For example, the word "dreams," which begins the sentence, is a word that conveys rich layers of meaning and mystery that did not exist prior to the publication of *The Interpretation of Dreams* (1900). Concentrated in this word newly created by Freud are allusions to (1) a conception of a repressed unconscious inner world that powerfully, but obliquely, exerts force on conscious experience, and vice versa; (2) a view that sexual desire is present from birth onward and is rooted in bodily instincts which manifest themselves in universal unconscious incestuous wishes, parricidal fantasies, and fears of retaliation in the form of genital mutilation; (3) a recognition of the role of dreaming as an essential conversation between unconscious and preconscious aspects of ourselves; and (4) a radical reconceptualization of human symbology – at once universal and exquisitely idiosyncratic to the life history of each individual. Of course, this list is only a sampling of the meanings that the word dream, newly made by Freud, invokes.

Similarly, the words "normal life," "mental disorders," and "narcissistic" speak to one another and to the word "dream" in ways that simply could not have occurred 20 years earlier. The second half of the sentence suggests that two other words denoting aspects of human experience will be made anew in this paper: "mourning" and "melancholia." (Freud's term melancholia is roughly synonymous with depression as the latter term is currently used.)

The logic of the central argument of "Mourning and melancholia" begins to unfold as Freud compares the psychological features of mourning to those of melancholia: both are responses to loss and involve "grave departures from the normal attitude to life" (p. 243). Freud comments that "it never occurs to us to regard [mourning] as a pathological condition and to refer it to medical treatment. We rely on its being overcome after a certain lapse of time, and we look upon any interference with it as useless or even harmful" (pp. 243–244). This observation is offered as a statement of the self-evident and may have been so in Vienna in 1915. But, to my mind, that understanding today is paid lip service far more often than it is genuinely honored.

In melancholia, one finds

> a profoundly painful dejection, cessation of interest in the outside world, loss of the capacity to love, inhibition of all activity, and a lowering of the self-regarding feelings to a degree that finds utterance in self-reproaches and self-revilings, and culminates in a delusional expectation of punishment.
>
> (p. 244)

Freud points out that the same traits characterize mourning – with one exception: "the disturbance of self-regard." Only in retrospect will the reader realize that the full weight of the thesis that Freud develops in this paper rests on this simple observation made almost in passing: "The disturbance of self-regard is absent in mourning; but otherwise the features are the same" (p. 244). As in every good detective novel, all clues necessary for solving the crime are laid out in plain view practically from the outset.

With the background of the discussion of the similarities and differences – there is only one symptomatic difference – between mourning and melancholia, the paper seems abruptly to plunge into the exploration of the unconscious. In melancholia, the patient and the analyst may not even know what the patient has lost – a remarkable idea from the point of view of common sense in 1915. Even when the melancholic is aware that he has suffered the loss of a person, "he knows *whom* he has lost but not *what* he has lost in him" (p. 245). There is ambiguity in Freud's language here. Is the melancholic unaware of the sort of importance the tie to the object held for him: "*what* [the melancholic] has lost in [losing] him." Or is the melancholic unaware of what he has lost *in himself* as a consequence of losing the object? The ambiguity – whether or not Freud intended it – subtly introduces the important notion of the simultaneity and interdependence of two unconscious aspects of object loss in melancholia. One involves the nature of the melancholic's tie to the object and the other involves an alteration of the self in response to the loss of the object.

> This [lack of awareness on the part of the melancholic of what he has lost] would suggest that melancholia is in some way related to an object-loss which is withdrawn from consciousness, in contradistinction to mourning, in which there is nothing about the loss that is unconscious.
>
> (p. 245)

In his effort to understand the nature of the unconscious object-loss in melancholia, Freud returns to the sole observable symptomatic difference between mourning and melancholia: the melancholic's diminished self-esteem.

> In mourning it is the world which has become poor and empty; in melancholia it is the ego itself. The patient represents his ego to us

15

as worthless, incapable of any achievement and morally despicable; he reproaches himself, vilifies himself and expects to be cast out and punished. He abases himself before everyone and commiserates with his own relatives for being connected with anyone so unworthy. He is not of the opinion that a change has taken place in him, but extends his self-criticism back over the past; he declares that he was never any better.

(p. 246)

More in his use of language than in explicit theoretical statements, Freud's model of the mind is being reworked here. There is a steady flow of subject–object, I–me pairings in this passage: the patient as subject reproaches, abases, vilifies himself as object (and extends the reproaches backward and forward in time). What is being suggested – and only suggested – is that these subject–object pairings extend beyond consciousness into the timeless unconscious and constitute what is going on unconsciously in melancholia that is not occurring in mourning. The unconscious is in this sense a metaphorical place in which the "I–me" pairings are unconscious psychological contents that actively engage in a continuous timeless attack by the subject (I) upon the object (me) which depletes the ego (a concept in transition here) to the point that it becomes "poor and empty" in the process.

The melancholic is ill in that he stands in a different relationship to his failings than does the mourner. The melancholic does not evidence the shame one would expect of a person who experiences himself as "petty, egoistic and dishonest" (p. 246), instead demonstrating an "insistent communicativeness which finds satisfaction in self-exposure" (p. 247). Each time Freud returns to the observation of the melancholic's diminished self-regard, he makes use of it to illuminate a different aspect of the unconscious "internal work" (p. 245) of melancholia. This time the observation, with its accrued set of meanings, becomes an important underpinning for a new conception of the ego, which up to this point has only been hinted at:

the melancholic's disorder affords [a view] of the constitution of the human ego. We see how in [the melancholic] one part of the ego sets itself over against the other, judges it critically, and, as it were, takes it as its object ... What we are here becoming acquainted with is the agency commonly called 'conscience' ...

16

and we shall come upon evidence to show that it can become diseased on its own account.

(p. 247)

Here, Freud is re-conceiving the ego in several important ways. These revisions taken together constitute the first of a set of tenets underlying Freud's emerging psychoanalytic theory of unconscious internal object relations: (1) The ego, now a psychic structure with conscious and unconscious components ("parts"), can be split; (2) an unconscious split-off aspect of the ego has the capacity to independently generate thoughts and feelings – in the case of the critical agency these thoughts and feelings are of a self-observing moralistic, judgmental sort; (3) a split-off part of the ego may enter into an unconscious relationship to another part of the ego; and (4) a split-off aspect of the ego may be either healthy or pathological.

Object-loss transformed into ego-loss

The paper becomes positively fugue-like in its structure as Freud takes up still again – yet in a new way – the sole symptomatic difference between mourning and melancholia:

If one listens patiently to a melancholic's many and various self-accusations, one cannot in the end avoid the impression that often the most violent of them are hardly at all applicable to the patient himself, but that with insignificant modifications they do fit someone else, someone whom the patient loves or has loved or should love ... So we find the key to the clinical picture: we perceive that the self-reproaches are reproaches against a loved object which have been shifted away from it on to the patient's own ego.

(p. 248)

Thus, Freud, as if developing enhanced observational acuity as he writes, sees something he previously had not noticed – that the accusations the melancholic heaps upon himself represent unconsciously displaced attacks on the loved object. This observation serves as a starting point from which Freud goes on to posit a second set of elements of his object relations theory.

17

In considering the melancholic's unconscious reproaches of the loved object, Freud picks up a thread that he had introduced earlier in the discussion. Melancholia often involves a psychological struggle involving ambivalent feelings for the loved object as "in the case of a betrothed girl who has been jilted" (p. 245). Freud elaborates on the role of ambivalence in melancholia by observing that melancholics show not the slightest humility despite their insistence on their own worthlessness "and always seem as though they felt slighted and had been treated with great injustice" (p. 248). Their intense sense of entitlement and injustice "is possible only because the reactions expressed in their behaviour still proceed from a mental constellation of revolt, which has then, by a certain process, passed over into the crushed state of melancholia" (p. 248).

It seems to me that Freud is suggesting that the melancholic experiences outrage (as opposed to anger of other sorts) at the object for disappointing him and doing him a "great injustice." This emotional protest/revolt is crushed in melancholia as a consequence of "a certain process." It is the delineation of that "certain process" in theoretical terms that will occupy much of the remainder of "Mourning and melancholia."

The reader can hear unmistakable excitement in Freud's voice in the sentence that follows: "There is no difficulty in reconstructing this [transformative] process" (p. 248). Ideas are falling into place. A certain clarity is emerging from the tangle of seemingly contradictory observations, for example, the melancholic's combination of severe self-condemnation and vociferous self-righteous outrage. In spelling out the psychological process mediating the melancholic's movement from revolt (against injustices he has suffered) to a crushed state, Freud, with extraordinary dexterity, presents a radically new conception of the structure of the unconscious:

> An object-choice, an attachment of the libido to a particular person, had at one time existed [for the melancholic]; then, owing to a real slight or disappointment coming from this loved person, the object relationship was shattered. The result was not the normal one of a withdrawal of the libido [loving emotional energy] from this object and a displacement of it on to a new one . . . [Instead,] the object-cathexis [the emotional investment in the object] proved to have little power of resistance [little capacity to maintain the tie to the object], and was brought to an end. But the

18

free libido was not displaced on to another object; it was with-drawn into the ego. There, . . . it [the loving emotional invest-ment which has been withdrawn from the object] served to establish an *identification* of [a part of] the ego with the abandoned object. Thus, the shadow of the object fell upon [a part of] the ego, and the latter could henceforth be judged by a special agency [another part of the ego], as though it were an object, the forsaken object. In this way an object-loss was transformed into an ego-loss [a diminution of one's self-regard] and the conflict between the ego and the loved person [was transformed] into a cleavage between the critical activity of [a part of] the ego [later to be called the superego] and the ego as altered by identification.

(pp. 248–249)

These sentences represent a powerfully succinct demonstration of the way Freud in this paper was beginning to write/think theoreti-cally and clinically in terms of relationships between unconscious, paired, split-off aspects of the ego (i.e. about unconscious internal object relations[1]). Freud, for the first time, is gathering together into a coherent narrative expressed in higher-order theoretical terms his newly conceived revised model of the mind.

There is so much going on in this passage that it is difficult to know where to start in discussing it. Freud's use of language seems to me to afford a port of entry into this critical moment in the develop-ment of psychoanalytic thought. There is an important shift in the language Freud is using that serves to convey a rethinking of an important aspect of his conception of melancholia. The words

---

1 While Freud made use of the idea of "an internal world" in "Mourning and melan-cholia," it was Klein (1935, 1940, 1952) who transformed the idea into a systematic theory of the structure of the unconscious and of the interplay between the internal object world and the world of external objects. In developing her conception of the unconscious, Klein richly contributed to a critical alteration of analytic theory. She shifted the dominant metaphors from those associated with Freud's topographic and structural models to a set of spatial metaphors (some stated, some only suggested in "Mourning and melancholia"). These spatial metaphors depict an unconscious inner world inhabited by "internal objects" – split-off aspects of the ego – that are bound together in "internal object relationships" by powerful affective ties. (See Chapters 3 and 4 for discussions of the concepts of "internal objects" and "internal object relations" as these ideas evolved in the work of Freud, Klein, Isaacs, and Fairbairn; see also Ogden, 1983.)

"object-loss," "lost object," and even "lost as an object of love," are, without comment on Freud's part, replaced by the words "abandoned object" and "forsaken object."

The melancholic's "abandonment" of the object (as opposed to the mourner's loss of the object) involves a paradoxical psychological event: the abandoned object, for the melancholic, is preserved in the form of an identification with it: "Thus [in identifying with the object] the shadow of the object fell upon the ego" (p. 249). In melancholia, the ego is altered not by the glow of the object, but (more darkly) by "the shadow of the object." The shadow metaphor suggests that the melancholic's experience of identifying with the abandoned object has a thin, two-dimensional quality as opposed to a lively, robust feeling tone. The painful experience of loss is short-circuited by the melancholic's identification with the object, thus denying the separateness of the object: the object is me and I am the object. There is no loss; an external object (the abandoned object) is omnipotently replaced by an internal one (the ego-identified-with-the-object).

So, in response to the pain of loss, the ego is twice split, forming an internal object relationship in which one split-off part of the ego (the critical agency) angrily (with outrage) turns on another split-off part of the ego (the ego-identified-with-the-object). Although Freud does not speak in these terms, it could be said that the internal object relationship is created for the purpose of evading the painful feeling of object loss. This avoidance is achieved by means of an unconscious "deal with the devil": in exchange for the evasion of the pain of object-loss, the melancholic is doomed to experience the sense of lifelessness that comes as a consequence of disconnecting oneself from large portions of external reality. In this sense, the melancholic forfeits a substantial part of his own life — the three-dimensional emotional life lived in the world of real external objects. The internal world of the melancholic is powerfully shaped by the wish to hold captive the object in the form of an imaginary substitute for it — the ego-identified-with-the-object. In a sense, the internalization of the object renders the object forever captive to the melancholic and at the same time renders the melancholic endlessly captive to it.

A dream of one of my patients comes to mind as a particularly poignant expression of the frozen quality of the melancholic's unconscious internal object world.

The patient, Mr. K, began analysis a year after the death of his wife of 22 years. In a dream that Mr. K reported several years into the analysis, he was attending a gathering in which a tribute was to be paid to someone whose identity was unclear to him. Just as the proceedings were getting under way, a man in the audience rose to his feet and spoke glowingly of Mr. K's fine character and important accomplishments. When the man finished, the patient stood and expressed his gratitude for the high praise, but said that the purpose of the meeting was to pay tribute to the guest of honor, so the group's attention should be directed to him. Immediately upon Mr. K's sitting down, another person stood and again praised the patient at great length. Mr. K again stood and after briefly repeating his statement of gratitude for the adulation, he re-directed the attention of the gathering to the honored guest. This sequence was repeated again and again until the patient had the terrifying realization (in the dream) that this sequence would go on forever. Mr. K awoke from the dream with his heart racing in a state of panic.

The patient had told me in the sessions preceding the dream that he had become increasingly despairing of ever being able to love another woman and "resume life." He said he has never ceased expecting his wife to return home after work each evening at six-thirty. He added that every family event after her death has been for him nothing more than another occasion at which his wife is missing. He apologized for his lugubrious, self-pitying tones.

I told Mr. K that I thought that the dream captured a sense of the way he feels imprisoned in his inability genuinely to be interested in, much less honor, new experiences with people. In the dream, he, in the form of the guests paying endless homage to him, directed to himself what might have been interest paid to someone outside of himself, someone outside of his internally frozen relationship with his wife. I went on to say that it was striking that the honored guest in the dream was not given a name, much less an identity and human qualities which might have stirred curiosity, puzzlement, anger, jealousy, envy, compassion, love, admiration or any other set of feeling responses to another person. I added that the horror he felt at the end of the dream seemed to reflect his awareness that the static state of self-imprisonment in which he lives is potentially endless. (A good deal of this interpretation referred back to many discussions Mr. K and I had had concerning his state of being "stuck" in a world that no longer existed.) Mr. K responded by telling me that as I was speaking he remembered another part of the dream made up of a single still image of himself wrapped in heavy chains, unable to move even a single muscle of his body. He said he felt repelled by the extreme passivity of the image.

The dreams and the discussion that followed represented something of a turning point in the analysis. The patient's response to separations from me between sessions and during weekend and holiday breaks became less frighteningly bleak for him. In the period following this session, Mr. K found that he sometimes could go for hours without experiencing the heavy bodily sensation in his chest that he had lived with unremittingly since his wife's death.

While the idea of the melancholic's unconscious identification with the lost/abandoned object for Freud held "the key to the clinical picture" (p. 248) of melancholia, Freud believed that the key to the theoretical problem of melancholia would have to satisfactorily resolve an important contradiction:

> on the one hand, a strong fixation [an intense, yet static emotional tie] to the loved object must have been present; on the other hand, in contradiction to this, the object-cathexis must have had little power of resistance [i.e. little power to maintain that tie to the object in the face of actual or feared death of the object or object-loss as a consequence of disappointment].
>
> (p. 249)

The "key" to a psychoanalytic theory of melancholia that resolves the contradiction of the co-existing strong fixation to the object and the lack of tenacity of that object-tie lies, for Freud, in the concept of narcissism: "this contradiction seems to imply that the object-choice has been effected on a narcissistic basis, so that the object-cathexis, when obstacles come in its way, can regress to narcissism" (p. 249).

Freud's theory of narcissism, which he had introduced only months earlier in his paper, "On narcissism: An introduction" (1914b), provided an important part of the context for the object relations theory of melancholia that he was developing in "Mourning and melancholia." In his narcissism paper, Freud proposed that the normal infant begins in a state of "original" or "primary" narcissism (p. 75), a state in which all emotional energy is ego libido, a form of emotional investment that takes the ego (oneself) as its sole object. The infant makes a step toward the world outside of himself in the form of narcissistic identification – a type of object tie that treats the external object as an extension of oneself.

From the intermediate position of narcissistic identification, the healthy infant, in time, develops sufficient psychological stability to engage in a narcissistic form of relatedness to objects in which the tie to the object is largely made up of a displacement of ego libido from the ego onto the object (Freud, 1914b).

> Thus we form the idea of there being an original libidinal cathexis of the ego, from which some [of the emotional investment in the ego] is later given off to objects, but [the emotional investment in the ego] . . . fundamentally persists and is related to the [narcissistic] object-cathexes, much as the body of an amoeba is related to the pseudopodia which it puts out.
>
> (ibid., p. 75)

In other words, a narcissistic object tie is one in which the object is invested with emotional energy that originally was directed at oneself (and, in that sense, the object is a stand-in for the self). The movement from narcissistic identification to narcissistic object tie is a matter of a small but significant shift in the degree of recognition of, and emotional investment in, the otherness of the object.

The healthy infant is then able to go on to achieve a differentiation of ego–libido and object–libido. In this process of differentiation, he is beginning to engage in a form of object love that is not simply a displacement of love of oneself onto the object. Instead, a more mature form of object love evolves in which the infant achieves relatedness to objects that are experienced as external to himself – outside the realm of the infant's omnipotence.

Herein lies for Freud the key to the theoretical problem – the "contradiction" – posed by melancholia: *melancholia is a disease of narcissism*. A necessary "pre-condition" (p. 249) for melancholia is a disturbance in early narcissistic development. The melancholic patient in infancy and childhood was unable to move successfully from narcissism to object-love. Consequently, in the face of object loss or disappointment, the melancholic is incapable of mourning, i.e. unable to face the reality of the loss of the object, and, over time, to enter into mature object love with another person. The melancholic does not have the capacity to disengage from the lost object and instead evades the pain of loss through regression from narcissistic object relatedness to narcissistic identification: "the result of which is that in spite of the conflict [disappointment leading to outrage] with the loved person, the love relation need not be given up" (p. 249). As Freud put it in a summary statement near the end of the paper, "So by taking flight into the ego [by means of a powerful narcissistic identification] love escapes extinction" (p. 247).

A misreading of "Mourning and melancholia," to my mind, has become entrenched in what is commonly held to be Freud's view of melancholia (see, for example, Gay, 1988, pp. 372–373). What I am referring to is the misconception that melancholia, according to Freud, involves an identification with the hated aspect of an ambivalently loved object that has been lost. Such a reading, while accurate so far as it goes, misses the central point of Freud's thesis. What differentiates the melancholic from the mourner is the fact that the melancholic all along has been able to engage only in narcissistic forms of object relatedness. The narcissistic nature of the melancholic's personality renders him incapable of maintaining a firm connection with the painful reality of the irrevocable loss of the object, which is necessary for mourning. Melancholia involves ready, reflexive recourse to regression to narcissistic identification as a way of not experiencing the hard edge of recognition of one's inability to undo the fact of the loss of the object.

Object relations theory, as it is taking shape in the course of Freud's writing this paper, now includes an early developmental axis. The world of unconscious internal object relations is being viewed by Freud as a defensive regression to very early forms of object relatedness in response to psychological pain – in the case of the melancholic, the pain is the pain of loss. The individual replaces what might have become a three-dimensional relatedness to the mortal and at times disappointing external object with a two-dimensional (shadow-like) relationship to an internal object that exists in a psychological domain outside of time (and consequently sheltered from the reality of death). In so doing, the melancholic evades the pain of loss, and, by extension, other forms of psychological pain, but does so at an enormous cost – the loss of a good deal of his own (emotional) vitality.

One unconscious part of the ego stalking another

Having hypothesized the melancholic's substitution of an unconscious internal object relationship for an external one, and having wed this to a conception of defensive regression to narcissistic identification, Freud turns to a third defining feature of melancholia which, as will be seen, provides the basis for another important feature of his psychoanalytic theory of unconscious internal object relationships:

> In melancholia, the occasions which give rise to the illness extend for the most part beyond the clear case of a loss by death, and include all those situations of being slighted, neglected or disappointed, which can import opposed feelings of love and hate into the relationship or reinforce an already existing ambivalence. . . . The melancholic's erotic cathexis [erotic emotional investment in the object] . . . has thus undergone a double vicissitude: part of it has regressed to [narcissistic] identification, but the other part, under the influence of the conflict due to ambivalence, has been carried back to the stage of sadism.
>
> (pp. 251–252)

Sadism is a form of object tie in which hate (the melancholic's outrage at the object) becomes inextricably intertwined with erotic love, and in this combined state can be an even more powerful binding force (in a suffocating, subjugating, tyrannizing way) than the ties of love alone. The sadism in melancholia – generated in response to the loss of or disappointment by a loved object – gives rise to a special form of torment for both the subject and the object: that particular mixture of love and hate encountered in stalking. In this sense, the sadistic aspect of the relationship of the critical agency to the split-off ego-identified-with-the-object might be thought of as a relentless, crazed stalking of one split-off aspect of the ego by another – what Fairbairn (1944) would later view as the love/hate bond between the libidinal ego and the exciting object (see Chapter 4).

This conception of the enormous binding force of combined love and hate is an integral part of the psychoanalytic understanding of the astounding durability of pathological internal object relations. Such allegiance to the bad (hated and hating) internal object is often the

25

source of both the stability of the pathological structure of the patient's personality organization, and of some of the most intractable transference–countertransference impasses that we encounter in analytic work. In addition, the bonds of love mixed with hate account for such forms of pathological relationships as the ferocious ties of the abused child and the battered spouse to their abusers (and the tie of the abusers to the abused). The abuse is unconsciously experienced by both abused and abuser as loving hate and hateful love – both of which are far preferable to no object relationship at all (Fairbairn, 1944).

The psychotic edge of mania and melancholia

Employing one of his favorite extended metaphors – the analyst as detective – Freud creates in his writing a sense of adventure, risk-taking and even suspense as he takes on "the most remarkable characteristic of melancholia, . . . its tendency to change round into mania – a state which is the opposite of it in its symptoms" (p. 258). Freud's use of language in his discussion of mania – which is inseparable from the ideas he presents – creates for the reader a sense of the fundamental differences between mourning and melancholia, and between healthy (internal and external) object relationships and pathological ones.

> I cannot promise that this attempt [to explain mania] will prove entirely satisfactory. It hardly carries us much beyond the possibility of taking one's initial bearings. We have two things to go upon: the first is a psycho-analytic impression, and the second what we may perhaps call a matter of general economic experience. The [psycho-analytic] impression . . . is that . . . both disorders [mania and melancholia] are wrestling with the same, [unconscious] 'complex', but that probably in melancholia the ego has succumbed to the complex [in the form of a painful feeling of having been crushed] whereas in mania it has mastered it [the pain of loss] or pushed it aside.
>
> (p. 253–254)

The second of the two things "we have . . . to go upon" is "general economic experience." In attempting to account for the feelings of exuberance and triumph in mania, Freud hypothesized that the economics of mania – the quantitative distribution and play of psychological forces – may be similar to those seen when

> some poor wretch, by winning a large sum of money, is suddenly relieved from chronic worry about his daily bread, or when a long and arduous struggle is finally crowned with success, or when a man finds himself in a position to throw off at a single blow some oppressive compulsion, some false position which he has long had to keep up, and so on.
>
> (p. 254)

Beginning with the pun on "economic conditions" in the description of the poor wretch who wins a great deal of money, the sentence goes on to capture something of the feel of mania in its succession of images which are unlike any other set of images in the article. These dramatic cameos suggest to me Freud's own understandable magical wishes to have his own "arduous struggle . . . finally crowned with success" or to be able "to throw off at a single blow [his own] . . . oppressive compulsion" to write prodigious numbers of books and articles in his efforts to attain for himself and psychoanalysis the stature they deserve. And like the inevitable end of the expanding bubble of mania, the driving force of the succession of images seems to collapse into the sentences that immediately follow:

> This explanation [of mania by analogy to other forms of sudden release from pain] certainly sounds plausible, but in the first place it is too indefinite, and, secondly, it gives rise to more new problems and doubts than we can answer. We will not evade a discussion of them, even though we cannot expect it to lead us to a clear understanding.
>
> (p. 255)

Freud – whether or not he was aware of it – is doing more than alerting the reader to his uncertainties regarding how to understand mania and its relation to melancholia; he is showing the reader in his use of language, in the structure of his thinking and writing, what it sounds like and feels like to think and write in a way that does not attempt to confuse what is omnipotently, self-deceptively, wished for with what is real; words are used in an effort to simply, accurately, clearly give ideas and situations their proper names.

27

Bion's work provides a useful context for understanding more fully the significance of Freud's comment that he will not "evade" the new problems and doubts to which his hypothesis gives rise. Bion (1962a) uses the idea of evasion to refer to what he believes to be a hallmark of psychosis: eluding pain rather than attempting to symbolize it for oneself (for example, in dreaming), live with it, and do genuine psychological work with it over time. The latter response to pain – living with it, symbolizing it for oneself, and doing psychological work with it – lies at the heart of the experience of mourning. In contrast, the manic patient who "master[s] the [pain of loss] . . . or push[es] it aside" (Freud, 1917a, p. 244) transforms what might become a feeling of terrible disappointment, aloneness and impotent rage into a state resembling "joy, exultation or triumph" (ibid., p. 254).

I believe that Freud, here, without explicit acknowledgment – and perhaps without conscious awareness – begins to address the psychotic edge of mania and melancholia. The psychotic aspects of both mania and melancholia involve the evasion of grief as well as a good deal of external reality. This is effected by means of multiple splittings of the ego in conjunction with the creation of a timeless imaginary internal object relationship which omnipotently substitutes for the loss of a real external object relationship. More broadly speaking, a fantasied unconscious internal object world replaces an actual external one, omnipotence replaces helplessness, immortality substitutes for the uncompromising realities of the passage of time and of death, triumph replaces despair, contempt substitutes for love.

Thus Freud (in part explicitly, in part implicitly, and perhaps in part unknowingly) through his discussion of mania adds another important element to his evolving object relations theory. The reader can hear in Freud's use of language (for example, in his comments on the manic patient triumphantly pushing aside the pain of loss and exulting in his imaginary victory over the lost object) the idea that the unconscious internal object world of the manic patient is constructed for the purpose of evading, "taking flight" (p. 257) from, the external reality of loss and death. This act of taking flight from external reality has the effect of plunging the patient into a sphere of omnipotent thinking cut off from life lived in relation to actual external objects. The world of external object relations becomes depleted as a consequence of its having been disconnected from the individual's unconscious internal object world. The patient's experience in the world of external objects is disconnected from the

28

enlivening "fire" (Loewald, 1978, p. 189) of the unconscious internal object world. Conversely, the unconscious internal object world, having been cut off from the world of external objects, cannot grow, cannot "learn from experience" (Bion, 1962a), and cannot enter (in more than a very limited way) into generative "conversations" between unconscious and preconscious aspects of oneself "at the frontier of dreaming" (Ogden, 2001).

The wish to continue living and the wish to be at one with the dead

Freud concludes the paper with a series of thoughts on a wide range of topics related to mourning and melancholia. Of these, his expansion of the concept of ambivalence is, I believe, the one that represents the most important contribution both to the understanding of melancholia and to the development of his object relations theory. Freud had discussed on many previous occasions, beginning as early as 1900, a view of ambivalence as an unconscious conflict of love and hate in which the individual unconsciously loves the same person he hates, for example, in the distressing ambivalence of healthy Oedipal experience or in the paralyzing torments of the ambivalence of the obsessional neurotic. In "Mourning and melancholia," Freud uses the term *ambivalence* in a strikingly different way; he uses it to refer to a struggle between the wish to live with the living and the wish to be at one with the dead:

> hate and love contend with each other [in melancholia]; the one seeks to detach the libido from the object [thus allowing the subject to live and the object to die], the other to maintain this position of the libido [which is bonded to the immortal internal version of the object].
>
> (p. 256)

Thus, the melancholic experiences a conflict between, on the one hand, the wish to be alive with the pain of irreversible loss and the reality of death, and on the other hand, the wish to deaden himself to the pain of loss and the knowledge of death. The individual capable of mourning succeeds in freeing himself from the struggle between life and death that freezes the melancholic: "mourning impels the ego to give up the object by declaring the object to be dead and offering the ego the inducement of continuing to live" (p. 257). So the mourner's painful acceptance of the reality of the death of the object is achieved in part because the mourner knows (unconsciously and, at times, consciously) that his own life, his own capacity for "continuing to live" is at stake.

I am reminded of a patient who began analysis with me almost 20 years after the death of her husband.

> Ms. G told me that not long after her husband's death, she had spent a weekend alone at a lake where for each of the 15 years prior to his death, she and her husband had rented a cabin. She told me that during a trip to the lake soon after his death, she had set out alone in a motorboat and headed toward a labyrinth of small islands and tortuous waterways that she and her husband had explored many times. Ms. G said that the idea had come to her with a sense of absolute certainty that her husband was in that set of waterways, and that if she were to have entered that part of the lake, she never would have come out because she would not have been able to "tear" herself away from him. She told me that she had had to fight with all her might not to go to be with her husband.
>
> That decision not to follow her husband into death became an important symbol in the analysis of the patient's choosing to live her life in a world filled with the pain of grief and her living memories of her husband. As the analysis proceeded, that same event at the lake came to symbolize something quite different: the incompleteness of her act of "tearing" herself away from her husband after his death. It became increasingly clear in the transference–countertransference that, in an important sense, a part of herself had gone with her husband into death, that is, an aspect of herself had been deadened, and that that had been "all right" with her until that juncture in the analysis.
>
> In the course of the subsequent year of analysis, Ms. G experienced a sense of enormous loss – not only the loss of her husband, but also the loss of her own life. She confronted for the first time the pain and sadness of the recognition of the ways she had for decades unconsciously limited herself with regard to utilizing her intelligence and artistic talents as well as her capacities to fully be alive in her everyday experience (including her analysis). (I do not view Ms. G as having been manic, or even as having relied heavily

on manic defenses, but I believe that she held in common with the manic patient a form of ambivalence that involves a tension between, on the one hand, the wish to live life among the living – internally and externally – and, on the other hand, the wish to exist with the dead in a timeless dead and deadening internal object world.)

Returning to Freud's discussion of mania, the manic patient is engaged in a "struggle of ambivalence [in a desperate unconscious effort to come to life through] . . . loosening the fixation of libido to the [internal] object by disparaging it, denigrating it and even as it were killing it" (p. 257).[2] This sentence is surprising: mania represents not only the patient's effort to evade the pain of grief by disparaging and denigrating the object. Mania also represents the patient's (often unsuccessful) attempts *to achieve grief* by freeing himself from the mutual captivity involved in the unconscious internal relationship with the lost object. In order to grieve the loss of the object, one must first kill it, that is, one must do the psychological work of allowing the object to be irrevocably dead, both in one's own mind and in the external world.

By introducing the notion of a form of ambivalence involving the struggle between the wish to go on living and the wish to deaden oneself in an effort to be with the dead, Freud added a critical dimension to his object relations theory: the notion that unconscious internal object relations may have either a living and enlivening quality or a dead and deadening quality (and by extension, every possible combination of the two). Such a way of conceiving the internal object world has been central to the developments in psychoanalytic theory pioneered by Winnicott (1971a) and Green (1983). These authors have placed emphasis on the importance of the analyst's and the patient's experiences of the aliveness and deadness of the

---

2 The reader can hear the voice of Melanie Klein (1935, 1940) in this part of Freud's comments on mania. All three elements of Klein's (1935) well-known clinical triad characterizing mania and the manic defense – control, contempt and triumph – can be found in nascent form in Freud's conception of mania. The object never will be lost or missed because it is, in unconscious fantasy, under one's omnipotent control, so there is no danger of losing it; even if the object were lost, it would not matter because the contemptible object is "valueless" (p. 257), and one is better off without it; moreover, being without the object is a "triumph" (p. 254), an occasion for "enjoy[ing]" (p. 257) one's emancipation from the burdensome albatross that has been hanging from one's neck.

31

patient's internal object world. The sense of aliveness and deadness of the transference–countertransference is, to my mind, perhaps the single most important measure of the status of the analytic process on a moment-to-moment basis (Ogden, 1995, 1997). The sound of much of current analytic thinking – and, I suspect, the sound of psychoanalytic thinking yet to be thought – can be heard in Freud's "Mourning and melancholia," if we know how to listen.

Freud closes the paper with a voice of genuine humility, breaking off his inquiry mid-thought:

> But here once again, it will be well to call a halt and to postpone any further explanation of mania . . . As we already know, the interdependence of the complicated problems of the mind forces us to break off every enquiry before it is completed – till the outcome of some other enquiry can come to its assistance.
>
> (p. 259)

How better to end a paper on the pain of facing reality and the consequences of attempts to evade it? The solipsistic world of a psychoanalytic theorist who is not firmly grounded in the reality of his lived experience with patients is very similar to the self-imprisoned melancholic who survives in a timeless, deathless (and yet deadened and deadening) internal object world.

Concluding comments

In presenting a reading of Freud's "Mourning and melancholia," I have examined not only the ideas that Freud was introducing, but also, as important, the way he was thinking/writing in this watershed paper. I have attempted to demonstrate how Freud made use of his exploration of the unconscious work of mourning and melancholia to propose and explore some of the major tenets of a revised model of the mind (which later would be termed *object relations theory*). The principal tenets of the revised model presented in this 1917 paper include: (1) the idea that the unconscious is organized to a significant degree around stable internal object relations between paired split-off parts of the ego; (2) the notion that psychic pain may be defended against by means of the replacement of an external object relationship by an unconscious, fantasized internal object relationship; (3) the idea that pathological bonds of love mixed with hate are among the strongest ties that bind internal objects to one another in a state of mutual captivity; (4) the notion that the psychopathology of internal object relations often involves the use of omnipotent thinking to a degree that cuts off the dialogue between the unconscious internal object world and the world of actual experience with real external objects; and (5) the idea that ambivalence in relations between unconscious internal objects involves not only conflict between feelings of love and hate, but also conflict between wishes to continue to be alive in one's object relationships and wishes to be at one with one's dead internal objects.

3

Reading Susan Isaacs

Toward a radically revised theory of thinking

Susan Isaacs was chosen by Klein to present the opening paper in the Controversial Discussions held by the British Psychoanalytical Society between 1941 and 1945. Almost 70 years later, Isaacs' contribution holds up not simply as an historical landmark in the development of a psychoanalytic theory of thinking, but as a critical part of contemporary analytic theory. Isaacs' paper, "The nature and function of phantasy" (pre-circulated and presented to the British Psychoanalytical Society on 27 January, 1943) is at the same time a "scientific" psychoanalytic paper (a paper that presents and develops an original idea that is accompanied by supporting evidence) and a political position paper – a paper intended to establish Klein as a disciple of Freud, and not a "heretic" (Steiner, 1991, p. 248) whose ideas so diverged from Freud's that her work no longer deserved to be viewed as psychoanalysis.

The version of Isaacs' paper that I will be discussing was published in *Developments in Psychoanalysis* (1952), a collection of papers written and edited by Klein and her "inner circle" of Isaacs, Heimann and Rivière. The original paper (Isaacs, 1943a) – much briefer than the 1952 version and structured quite differently – does, at times, express ideas more compellingly than the 1952 version. I will cite such passages in the earlier version of the paper when they elucidate ideas being developed in the later one.

A good deal of the importance of Isaacs' (1952) contribution lies in her groundbreaking conception of the work of phantasy, which she clearly and systematically presents. And yet I find that much of what makes Isaacs' contribution pivotal to the development of psychoanalytic theory in the twentieth and twenty-first centuries

34

resides in what is only implicit in her paper. Specifically, it seems to me that Isaacs does not fully recognize that her paper is not a paper about the nature and function of phantasy, but a paper about the nature and the function of phantasying, that is, it is a paper primarily about thinking as opposed to a paper about thoughts. I attempt in my discussion of Isaacs' paper to extend ideas that she introduces in light of subsequent contributions to analytic thinking.

It seems to me that Isaacs' conception of the role of phantasy in the internal world contributes to a profound revision of the central psychoanalytic metaphors for the workings of the mind, that is, the replacement of Freud's structural model with a model of an inner world structured by phantasied internal object relationships. Moreover, I view Isaacs' contribution as anticipating aspects of Bion's (1962a, 1962b) theory of thinking. What I attempt to do in this paper is explicate the radical nature of Isaacs' revision of analytic theory, and, at the same time, articulate what Isaacs knew, but did not know that she knew. What makes for a timeless paper in any discipline is the way in which it is not only an original statement of present understandings, but also constitutes a memoir of the future. Isaacs' paper, to my mind, is such a paper.

Isaacs' aims and methodology

Isaacs (1952) indicates at the outset that she "is mostly concerned with the definition of 'phantasy' " (p. 67), and "is not primarily concerned to establish any particular content of phantasy" (p. 68); instead, she will address "the nature and function of phantasy as a whole, and its place in the mental life" (p. 68). While she intends to demonstrate that "the activity of phantasy [occurs] from the beginning of life" (p. 69), she recognizes that this "does not automatically imply accepting any particular phantasy content at any given age" (p. 69). Thus, Isaacs refuses to get mired in the controversy concerning *what* the infant is thinking or when a particular phantasy first occurs, but instead focuses on "the activity of phantasy," an activity that I believe is more accurately expressed in the form of a verb – *phantasying.*

The crux of the difficulty involved in proposing a conception of the unconscious phantasying activity of an infant lies in the fact that the infant cannot tell us what he is thinking, feeling, or imagining. "Our views about [unconscious] phantasy in these earliest years are based almost wholly upon inference, but then this is true at any age" (p. 69). All that one can know about the unconscious is, by definition, apprehended exclusively by inference. Consequently, the intellectual rigor of the methodology used in making such inferences is of critical importance.

Isaacs' (1952) inferences are made on the basis of three principles that she articulates: (1) "the need to attend to the precise *details* of a child's behaviour" (p. 70); (2) "the principle of noting and recording the *context of observed data* . . . the whole immediate setting of the behaviour being studied, in its social and emotional situation" (p. 71), for example, the external reality with which the infant is interacting; and (3) the principle of "*genetic continuity*" (p. 74).

The third of these principles holds a place of special importance in the construction of Isaacs' argument. She demonstrates that the development of a child's physical capacities and mental functions (for example, learning to speak and to walk) can be observed to have their origins in earliest infancy. Speech development begins with the earliest sounds the infant makes (for instance, when he is hungry or feeding) and develops by means of a combination of continuous growth and of "crises" (p. 74), such as the child's achieving the capacity to speak its first words.

The principle of genetic continuity is critical to Isaacs' argument that the infant begins to generate unconscious phantasies from the earliest days of life.

> *The established principle of genetic continuity is a concrete instrument of knowledge.* It enjoins upon us to accept no particular facts of behaviour or mental processes as *sui generis*, ready-made, or suddenly emerging, but to regard them as items in a developing series. We seek to trace them backwards through earlier and more rudimentary stages to their most germinal forms . . .
>
> (p. 75)

Isaacs here invokes the principle of genetic continuity in order to lend support to a methodology that makes inferences about the nature of unconscious phantasy in the earliest days of life on the basis of data drawn, for example, from child analysis and symbolic play occurring much later in the life of the child. A weakness in Isaacs' argument lies in the fact that while she recognizes that there is a constant tension between continuity and discontinuity in physical and psychological

36

development, she places far greater emphasis on continuity than on disjunction in development. In so doing, she underplays the importance of such phenomena as the quantum leaps in the evolution of the morphology of every species, for example, the transformation that takes place in butterfly larvae when their specialized organs break down and give rise to undifferentiated clusters of cells that organize themselves into "imaginal discs." "Their spurt of growth now shapes the organism according to a new plan. New organs arise from the discs" (Karp and Berrill, 1981, p. 692). Thus, the morphology and physiology of the mature butterfly is discontinuous from the morphology and much of the physiology of the caterpillar while the DNA of the caterpillar and the butterfly remain identical.

Similarly, in infantile development, Spitz (1965) points out that the infant evidences not only developmental continuity, but also quantum leaps in psychological development due to psychic reorganizations that are reflected, for instance, in the virtually overnight appearance of the infant's smiling response at about three months, separation anxiety at about seven months and the capacity for a yes/no response at 14 months. With regard to the appearance of the smiling response, for example, there can be no mistaking that an enormous developmental transformation has occurred in which the infant has become capable of forms of experience, qualities of thinking, types of communication, and forms of object relatedness that had not previously been part of his psychic life. Such transformations do not involve gradual progression; rather, they involve striking discontinuities that make it impossible to "trace backwards" (Isaacs, 1952, p. 77), to deduce the nature of earlier psychological capacities and states of mind on the basis of later ones. In other words, observation of the infant capable of smiling does not make it possible to make inferences about the psychological organization and mental processes characterizing an earlier stage of the mental life of the infant.

I will now turn to a second aspect of the assumptions underlying Isaacs' methodology. Reflecting the predominant thinking of her time, the methodology upon which Isaacs relies to infer the nature of early infantile unconscious phantasy involves viewing the infant's mental life as operating "within the infant" even though she acknowledges that the infant's mental state is responsive to events occurring in external reality. In her statement of methodology, Isaacs (1952) emphasizes the importance of observing both "precise *details*" (p. 70) and "*context*" (p. 71) for making inferences regarding the infant's internal world and its mental processes. The principal "context" of the life of the infant is maternal care, which is consistently treated by Isaacs as an event to which the infant is responding, rather than as an experience in which the mother *actively participates with the infant in generating the infant's internal life.*

Isaacs, who died in 1948 (at the age of 63), did not have available to her the concept of the mother–infant as a single psychological unit (in tension with the mother and infant as separate entities), a concept that Winnicott (1960) introduced in the form of his idea that "there is no such thing as an infant" [apart from the maternal provision] (p. 39 fn) and, at the same time, the mother and infant are distinctly separate people. Bion (1959) and Rosenfeld (1965) cast their own understandings of the mother–infant relationship in the form of their conceptions of projective identification as an unconscious, psycho-logical-interpersonal process through which mother and infant engage in thinking together (while remaining separate entities) beginning in earliest infancy. Consequently, Isaacs' understanding of infantile phantasy is cast almost entirely in terms of a conception of the mind of the infant as a system independent of, but responsive to, the workings of the mind of the mother. For Bion, Rosenfeld and Winnicott, as well as those influenced by their revision of the analytic conception of the mind of the infant, the development of the psycho-logical life of the infant is conceived not only in terms of the indi-vidual maturational advances of the infant, but also in terms of a psyche jointly created by mother and infant. From this perspective, the infant's earliest unconscious phantasies draw on the primitively organized mental state of the infant, on the mature psychological life of the mother, and on the interplay between the two. So, while Isaacs (1952) viewed attention to precise detail and to context as two of her methodological principles of infant observation, she was not able to include in her thinking the way in which the mother-as-context includes not only the mother as the surround of the infant, but also the mother as part of jointly constructed aspects of the work-ings (the metaphorical interior) of the infant's mind.

Phantasy as unconscious thinking

Isaacs (1952) then turns her attention to her greatly expanded concep-tion of unconscious phantasy. I speak of Isaacs's conception of phantasy, as opposed to Klein's conception, because I believe that Isaacs was, in many ways, a better analytic theorist than was Klein. (Klein [1946, 1955], for example, was never able to offer a definition of projective identification with the clarity and detail that Isaacs brings to her definition of phantasy.) Rivière (1952), in countering the idea that Isaacs' understanding of phantasy was, to a large extent, her own original contribution, stated that Isaacs' conception of phantasy "was consistently taken for granted by Klein throughout her work" (p. 16, fn 1). I find this a telling comment. There is a vast difference between taking an idea "for granted" and carefully, systematically explicating and developing an idea, garnering evidence for it, and spelling out its implications for other aspects of analytic theory, all of which Isaacs does in her paper.

For purposes of clarity, I will discuss separately a number of aspects of what I see as original and groundbreaking in Isaacs' contribution. In reality, these "aspects" are inseparable parts of a whole. What for Freud were " 'mental mechanisms' – by which impulses and feelings are controlled and expressed" (Isaacs, 1952, p. 78) are, for Isaacs, "particular sorts of phantasy" (p. 78). This understanding of the role of phantasy (more accurately, phantasying) in unconscious psychological life constitutes a turning point in the development of analytic theory. Isaacs conceives of all "mental processes" and "mental mechanisms" as forms of unconscious phantasying. In other words "mental operations" and "mechanisms" are not impersonal operations akin to the production of insulin by specialized cells in the pancreas in response to changes in blood sugar levels; rather, the various "mental mechanisms," such as the defense mechanisms described by Anna Freud (1936), are now to be viewed as personal psychological creations: "particular sorts of phantasy" (Isaacs, 1952, p. 78) that are unique to each individual.

For me, Isaacs' phrase "particular sorts of phantasy" constitutes at once a brilliant insight and the unfinished theoretical work of her paper. Isaacs' idea that mental mechanisms and operations are specific (unconscious) personal phantasies, to my mind, constitutes a transition from the "Freud–Klein era" to the "Winnicott–Bion era" of psychoanalysis (Ogden, 2010). In the "Freud–Klein era," the focus of psychoanalysis is primarily on understanding *what we think* (the symbolic content of unconscious thoughts, as reflected, for example, in dreams, play, and the analysand's associations). In the "Winnicott–Bion era," the primary focus is on *the ways we think* (our various forms of thinking and our inability to think, which are reflected, for example, in dreaming, playing, and imagining, as well as in the psychotic state of not being able to think). (Clearly, the emphasis of the latter "era" does not replace that of the earlier one; it supplements it.) This transitional function of Isaacs' paper constitutes, for me, the principal importance of the paper despite the fact that I do not believe that Isaacs was fully aware (perhaps not at all aware) of this implication of her work. Isaacs' (1952) use of language reflects the way in which she has one foot in each of the two "eras" of psychoanalysis. The fact that Isaacs uses the noun *phantasy* far more often than she uses the phrase *phantasy activity* (and rarely uses the verb *phantasying*) reflects her tie to the earlier era; on the other hand, her repeated use of the term *phantasy activity*, though a nominative phrase, reflects her expansion of the term *phantasy* to include not only mental content, but also unconscious mental action (i.e. thinking).

Having reconceived mental processes and mechanisms as unconscious phantasy activity, Isaacs, in a second major expansion of the concept of phantasy, focuses on a pivotal aspect of the practice of child and adult analysis: "the transference situation" (Isaacs, 1952, p. 78). "*[T]he patient's relation to his analyst is almost entirely one of unconscious phantasy . . .* the 'transference' has turned out to be the chief instrument of learning what is going on in the patient's mind, as well as of discovering or reconstructing his early history" (p. 79). Here Isaacs discusses the idea that transference *is* phantasy, an unconscious psychic construction based on early experience. I believe that this idea forms the basis for an even more fundamental development in our current understanding of transference: if transference is phantasying, and phantasying is unconscious thinking, then transference holds significance not simply as a symbolic expression of internal object relationships originating in infancy and childhood. In addition, transference, as I understand it, constitutes a *way of thinking for the first time* (in relation to the analyst) an emotional situation that occurred in the past. Transference, from this perspective, is inherently more verb than noun, that is, it comprises an effort to think disturbing experiences with the analyst that had previously been unthinkable.

In viewing transference in this way, I am bringing aspects of Winnicott's work to bear on my reading of Isaacs. I am drawing on Winnicott's (1974) concept of "fear of breakdown" (p. 90) – fear of psychological collapse that has already occurred much earlier in the patient's life (usually in infancy or childhood). When the breakdown occurred, the individual was not psychologically able (even with the help of his parents) to "encompass something" (Winnicott, 1974, p. 91), to take in what was occurring. The breakdown that has already occurred persists from that point on as a sense of impending psychological collapse: "the original experience of primitive agony cannot get into the past tense unless the ego can first gather it into its own present time experience" (Winnicott, 1974, p. 91). In the course of analysis, it may be possible for the patient, for the first time, to experience (in the context of the safety of the analytic relationship) an emotional event that had occurred much earlier in his life, but was too disturbing for him to experience at the time. *Transference activity, from this perspective, is a psychological act not of reliving infantile and childhood experience but, rather, the opposite of repetition of early experience – it is an act of experiencing for the first time (with the analyst and in relation to the analyst) an emotional event that occurred in infancy or childhood, but was impossible to experience at the time.* Thus, here, and in other parts of this paper, I find that knowledge of Winnicott's work enhances my reading of Isaacs no less than knowledge of Isaacs' work enriches my reading of Winnicott.

Phantasy as unconscious psychic reality

At this point in Isaacs' paper, the meaning of the term *phantasy* has (largely implicitly) been extended to include both unconscious psychic content and unconscious thinking. But this is just one aspect of Isaacs' expansion of the meaning of the term *phantasy*. She now goes on to say that Klein (and Freud) used the word *phantasy* to refer to *unconscious* mental activity (a fact that Strachey underscored by using the *ph* spelling of phantasy in the English translation). The reality of unconscious experience has "its *own objectivity as a mental fact*" (Isaacs, 1952, p. 81). In other words, psychic "reality" (the reality of unconscious phantasy) is no less real than external reality. Isaacs offers here a brilliantly lucid explanation of the emphasis that Kleinians place on the reality of unconscious phantasy – it is not "'merely' or 'only' imagined, as something unreal, in contrast with what is actual" (p. 81).

The idea that phantasy is the psychic reality of the unconscious leads, to my mind, to a new understanding of both phantasy and the unconscious. Isaacs introduces her view of phantasy and unconscious psychic reality by means of a description of Freud's view of the unconscious: it is an "inner world of the mind [that] has a continuous living reality of its own, with its own dynamic laws and characteristics, different from those of the external world" (Isaacs, 1952, p. 81). I believe that Isaacs' rendering of Freud's conception of the unconscious suggests a further meaning of phantasy that goes beyond the idea of phantasy as unconscious mental content and unconscious thinking. It seems to me that Freud's notion of the unconscious (as viewed by Isaacs) constitutes the beginnings of the idea that phantasy is a name given to a quality of reality that is characteristic of the unconscious mind. What I mean by this is that phantasy might be thought of as a way of thinking that has its own distinctive quality of reality, a reality that we experience as different from external reality (reality that is external to the mind, reality that we have not invented). The experience of external reality (conscious psychic reality) would not exist as an experience if it did not stand in tension with the experience of the unconscious psychic reality of phantasy. In other words, the experience of the reality of external reality would not exist in the absence of the experience, not of unreality, but of the unconscious reality of phantasy activity. The unconscious psychic reality of phantasy is a dimension of the totality of the reality of the experience of being alive. To put it in still other terms, the unconscious psychic reality of phastasy is that "invisible" quality of being alive out of which dreams come and into which dreams "disappear." From this perspective, "psychic reality" is a single experiential entity with multiple qualities, one of which involves conscious awareness, another of which does not. Neither quality of reality exists in isolation from the other: the two are qualities of a unitary experience.

Phantasy, symbolic meaning and unconscious self-reflection

Isaacs, in the 1943 version of her paper, quotes and endorses Rivière's (1936) definition of phantasy as "the subjective interpretation of experience" (Isaacs, 1943a, p. 41). This conception of phantasy holds profound significance with regard to the way one understands unconscious mental life. If phantasying (unconscious thinking) is the "subjective *interpretation* of experience" in both the internal and external object worlds, phantasying necessarily involves both a perceiving aspect of self and an aspect of self that interprets (is capable of rendering symbolically meaningful) what one is experiencing. Rendering one's experience symbolically meaningful is entirely different from responding (e.g. fearfully or boldly) to an experience. For example, ethologists have demonstrated that chicks only a few days old – which have never seen any other species of animal – are capable of differentiating between the wing patterns of predatory birds and those of non-predators. On sighting a real or simulated predatory wing pattern, the chicks scurry for cover (Lorenz, 1937; Tinbergen, 1957). This constitutes an instinctual recognition of, and response to, "a sign" in that the wing pattern holds a one-to-one correspondence to the predatory bird. The response to a sign constitutes an altogether different form of thinking from that involved in interpreting symbols and attributing personal meanings to them (for example, attributing personal meaning to the sight of a child waiting at a street corner). Phantasying, for Isaacs (and for Rivière), is an interpretive act and as such involves an interpreting subject who mediates between what one is perceiving (for example, a real child on a street corner or the image of a child in a dream) and the (unconscious) personal symbolic meanings (i.e. the phantasies) one creates from one's perception.

Isaacs is very clear that phantasy and meaning are inseparable. Phantasy is the process that creates meaning and the form in which meaning exists in unconscious mental life:

> The special character of mental as compared with physical processes is that they have *meaning*. Physical processes are said to have existence, but not *meaning* ... The word 'phantasy' serves to remind us always of this distinctive character of meaning in the [unconscious] mental life.
>
> (Isaacs, 1943a, p. 272)

Having introduced the idea that unconscious phantasy involves interpreting one's experience, Isaacs goes on to offer a detailed description of her conception of the way in which the infant deals with his experience psychically:

> The hungry or longing or distressed infant feels actual sensations in his mouth or his limbs or his viscera, which *mean to him* that certain things are being done to him or that he is doing such and such as

he wishes, or fears. He *feels as if* he were doing so and so – *e.g.* touching or sucking or biting the breast which is actually out of reach. Or he feels as if he were being forcibly and painfully deprived of the breast, or as if *it* were biting *him*; and this, at first, probably without visual or other plastic images.

(1952, p. 92)

Isaacs uses the words "*mean to him*" and "*feels as if*" six times in the space of three sentences. Isaacs, a lecturer in logic and child development (King, 1991, p. xv), uses the utmost care and thought in her choice of words. Her use of language, to my mind, reflects an awareness of the fact that in order to generate the qualities of experience that she is describing, there must be at least the rudiments of the capacity for operating on the basis of the reality principle. This impression is borne out a few paragraphs later when Isaacs states, "The earliest phantasies . . . are bound up with an actual, however limited and narrow, experience of objective reality" (p. 93). The capacity to recognize external reality allows the individual to compare one set of representations of experience with another, that is, to compare phantasy-generated experience with the perception and recognition of what one has not created (external reality).

To my ear, the language Isaacs uses also suggests that phantasy activity constitutes the beginnings of conscious and unconscious symbolic functioning in which experience is meaningful to an interpreting/understanding subject (it "mean[s] to him"). The experience she is describing is not simply that of a psychic presentation (a "thing in itself" [Barros and Barros, 2009]), but also, to some degree, an experience of feeling "as if," that is, an experience in which an interpreting subject differentiates between one form of reality (the reality of phantasy) and another (external reality) – this feels *like* that, but is *not* that.

To put this in other words, in order for unconscious phantasy to hold meaning of the sort that Isaacs is describing, it must mean something to someone who is an interpreting subject capable of differentiating between symbol and symbolized, between internal and external reality, between thought and what is being thought about. It seems to me that phantasy activity, conceived of in this way, is the mental activity that generates not only psychic content, unconscious thinking, and unconscious psychic reality, but also generates a state of consciousness in which that psychic content holds meaning *for*

44

oneself, beginning in earliest infancy. Though Isaacs never makes this explicit, to my mind, her conception of phantasying as an interpretive activity necessarily includes in the experience of unconscious thinking (phantasying) the beginnings of the experience of observing oneself and thinking about oneself (which is contingent on the capacity to experientially differentiate internal reality, external reality, and oneself as a subject mediating between the two).

Isaacs' (largely implicit) idea that phantasying involves unconscious interpretation/understanding of one's experience (both of the inner world and external reality) anticipates Sandler's (1976) idea that there is not only an unconscious "dream-work," but also an unconscious "understanding-work," and Grotstein's (2000) notion that there is not only an unconscious "dreamer who dreams the dream," but also an unconscious "dreamer who understands the dream." Sandler and Grotstein make explicit the idea that unconscious psychological work requires a form of unconscious self-reflection, an idea that I find implicit in Isaacs for the reasons I have stated, although she may not have ever consciously formulated that idea in these terms.

On another front, Isaacs conceives of the unconscious as characterized by the coexistence of primitive (for example, "symbolic equation" [Segal, 1957, p. 393]) and more mature forms of thinking and symbolizing (for example, "symbol formation proper" [Segal, 1957, p. 395]). This understanding of unconscious mental life foreshadows two of Bion's most important contributions: his conception of the healthy dialectical interplay of the paranoid-schizoid and depressive positions (Bion, 1962a) and his notion of the coexistence (in health and in psychopathological states) of the psychotic and non-psychotic parts of the personality (Bion, 1957).

Phantasy and psychic development

Another of the original contributions Isaacs makes in her discussion of phantasy is in the area of the relationship of phantasy to the development of the mind as a whole. As discussed earlier, Isaacs believes that phantasy is not simply the "mental expression" of instinct. In addition, "All impulses, all feelings, all modes of defence [much of which presents itself in sensory/bodily form] are experienced in phantasies which give them *mental life* and show their direction and purpose" (Isaacs, 1952, p. 83). It seems to me that this aspect of

Isaacs' conception of the role of phantasy – that of transforming sensory/bodily experience into elements of "mental life" – anticipates Bion's (1962b) concept of alpha function. Alpha function is an as yet unknown set of mental operations (a form of thinking) that transforms raw sense impressions into elements of experience (alpha-elements) that can be linked in the process of dreaming, which, for Bion (1962a), is synonymous with unconscious thinking. For Isaacs (1952), instinct – a bodily event that is experienced at first in sensory form – must undergo a transformation before being "experienced as phantasies which give them *mental life*" (p. 83). While Isaacs does not name that transformative function, her concept of phantasy activity is, I believe, akin to Bion's alpha function, i.e. phantasying is a mental function (a form of thinking) that transforms sense impressions associated with instinct into a mental form that can be linked to create personal, psychological meaning. An important difference between Isaacs' concept of phantasying and Bion's alpha function lies in the fact that, for Isaacs, the raw sense impressions that are transformed derive largely from instinct, while, for Bion (1962a), the raw sense impressions derive from lived emotional experience in the internal and external world.

Isaacs, without calling attention to it, makes use of her descriptions and interpretations of early infantile mental life to demonstrate the role of phantasying in still other forms of psychological development, including self–object differentiation. On the basis of infant observation and the data drawn from child analysis, Isaacs offers examples of what she hypothesizes to be the earliest phantasy experiences of the infant:

> When the child shows his desire for his mother's breast, he *experiences* this desire as a specific phantasy – 'I want to suck the nipple'. If desire is very intense (perhaps on account of anxiety), he is likely to feel: 'I want to eat her all up.'
>
> (Isaacs, 1952, p. 84)

Isaacs makes clear that while she is describing this phantasy in words, the infant's phantasies emerge from what W. C. M. Scott calls the "primary whole of experience, which is that of sucking-sensing-feeling-phantasying" (Scott's response to Isaacs' 1943 paper, quoted in Isaacs, 1952, p. 93, fn 2).

In this and many other passages, Isaacs points out that

these early mental processes [phantasies] have an omnipotent character . . . the child in his earliest days not only feels: 'I want to', but implicitly phantasies: 'I am doing' this and that to his mother; 'I *have* her inside me', when he wants to. The wish . . . tends to be felt as actually fulfilling itself whether with an external or an internal object.

(1952, p. 85)

But, at the same time, the wish is felt to be unfulfilled – as measured by the infant's nascent awareness of hunger, emptiness, loneliness, fear, and so on. In other words, the infant bumps up against external reality and the limits of his omnipotent thinking.

What is striking here is the simultaneity of two forms of thinking: omnipotent phantasying and thinking that recognizes the need to work with external reality (to think in the terms of non-magical, causal relationships presented by external reality). Even in the act of thinking omnipotently, there is a strong sense of "I-ness" and otherness in Isaacs' depiction of early phantasy activity. We find here a hallmark of Isaacs' thinking about the complexity inherent to the nature of phantasy: phantasy from the outset, in one sense, involves subject–object differentiation – "'I am doing' this and that to his mother." But, at the same time, in another sense, since the early phantasies are omnipotent in nature, they necessarily involve poor differentiation of self and object – the object is an extension of the subject, and so the object will do whatever the subject wants it to do. In its earliest days, the infant's "own wishes and impulses fill the whole world" (Isaacs, 1952, p. 85). To lose sight of either aspect of this set of dialectically constituted experiences of self and object – the experience of differentiated self and object and the experience of undifferentiated self and object – is to lose touch with the sophistication of Isaacs' thinking regarding forms of object relating mediated by phantasy activity that occurs in the early mental life of the infant.

Another aspect of psychic development in which phantasying plays a central role is the increasingly complex interplay of the reality of internal life and external reality. As I mentioned above, for Isaacs (1952), "phantasy thinking" (p. 108) does not stand in contrast with "reality thinking" (p. 108). Rather, phantasying always involves subjective interpretation of experience *and* a capacity for thinking informed by the reality principle: "In our view, *reality-thinking cannot operate without concurrent and supporting unconscious phantasies*" (Isaacs,

1952, p. 109). Phantasying always involves inextricably intertwined "subjective" and "objective" experience:

> The earliest phantasies, then, spring from bodily impulses and are interwoven with bodily sensations and affects. They express primarily an internal and subjective reality, yet from the beginning they are bound up with an actual, however limited and narrow, experience of objective reality.
>
> (p. 93)

Psychic development involves the creation of increasingly rich ways in which subjective reality and objective reality are "bound up with" one another. (I find Isaacs' phrase "bound up with" to be remarkable in its power to express a complex theoretical idea in ordinary language.) If there were no capacity for the "experience of objective reality," the infant's phantasying would not be grounded in anything beyond itself (that is, outside of phantasy). Omnipotent thinking would endlessly spin out of control without external reality to put "brakes" (Winnicott, 1945, p. 153) on it. No thinking process could "progress" in the sense of developing in a way that is informed by the constraints of, and interplay with, reality. Psychological maturation, in general, and the development of the capacity for thinking, in particular, requires, for example, that phantasies of omnipotent control over the breast and its supply of milk bump up against, and be modified by, the reality of hunger (which omnipotent phantasies cannot satisfy). In the absence of the infant's (or adult's) "actual . . . experience of objective reality" (Isaacs, 1952, p. 93), no maturation of conscious and unconscious thinking can occur.

Phantasy and knowledge of reality

Having discussed Isaacs' conception of the interplay of subjective and objective reality, there remains a major theoretical problem that Isaacs must address having to do with the source of knowledge inherent in the content of the phantasies she is attributing to the infant. Isaacs is well aware of the problem and addresses it directly:

> It has sometimes been suggested that unconscious phantasies such as that of 'tearing to bits' would not arise in the child's mind before

he had gained the conscious knowledge that tearing a person to bits [by biting and tearing] would mean killing him or her. Such a view does not meet the case. It overlooks the fact that such knowledge is *inherent* in bodily impulses as a vehicle of instinct, in the *aim* of instinct, in the excitation of the organ, *i.e.* in this case, the mouth.

(1952, pp. 93–94)

Isaacs is not proposing that knowledge of the workings of the external world is present at birth (the Lamarckian fallacy); rather, that "knowledge is *inherent* in bodily impulses" (Isaacs, 1952, p. 94). I would suggest that Isaacs is here adumbrating developments in linguistics, most prominently Chomsky's (1957, 1968) notion of the deep structure of language. Chomsky proposes that we do not inherit the capacity for speech, but we do inherit, in biological form, the deep structure of language which serves to organize sensory experience (the perception of the sounds of speech) into a language that has a grammatical structure and the potential to be used to create verbally symbolic speech as well as the capacity for reading and writing. Freud (1916–17), like Isaacs, proposes that there is a set of universal "primal phantasies" (pp. 370–371) (for example, the threat of castration and the seduction of children). But neither Freud nor Isaacs could account for the way in which the knowledge of external reality that is inherent in "primal phantasies" and "bodily impulses" is acquired in the absence of experience in the real world.

From a structuralist vantage point, it becomes quite plausible that "knowledge" (for example, the idea that tearing a person to bits with one's mouth will kill him or her) is inherent in bodily impulses, that is, in instincts that are constituted in part by a deep structure (templates) that serves to organize experience along particular lines. For example, for an infant or a small child, a bowel movement thrown away in a diaper by the mother or flushed down the toilet may serve as sensory (visual, tactile, olfactory, kinaesthetic, and auditory) forms lending themselves to be organized in terms of a biologically determined psychic template: the phantasy of the loss of a body part. Human beings are born with innumerable psychic templates with which experience is organized. For example, the wavelengths of light are organized by the brain into clusters that we see as different colors, even though there is no such grouping inherent in the evenly distributed range of wavelengths of light reaching the retina

49

(Bornstein, 1975). Isaacs' (as well as Freud's and Klein's) conception of phantasy seems to me to require a concept analogous to that of the deep structure of language in order to account for the universality of specific constellations of meanings (such as the Oedipus complex) which are integral parts of the psychoanalytic conception of universal human experience (Ogden, 1986).

Phantasy and the need to know

Isaacs' conception of phantasying is deeply rooted in Klein's (1930) concept of the epistemophilic instinct and in the relation of that impulse to symbol formation. (Isaacs makes specific reference to "the epistemophilic impulse" [p. 304] in the 1943 version of her paper, but, puzzlingly, does not do so in the 1952 version.) In the final portion of her 1952 paper, Isaacs develops the idea that the symbolic function of phantasy "builds a bridge from the inner world to interest in the outer world and knowledge of physical objects and events" (1952, p. 110). Phantasying promotes and sustains "the development of interest in the external world and the process of learning about it" (p. 110). "The power to seek out and organize knowledge [of the external world] is drawn" (p. 110) from phantasy activity. So, it could be said that, for Isaacs, a major force driving phantasy activity (unconscious thinking) is the need to get to know the real world, both external and internal, and one's relation to it. Phantasy is a principal vehicle for what Saul Bellow (2000) calls that "deep human need . . . for reading reality – the impulse to put your loving face to it and press your hands against it" (p. 203).

Bion (1962a, 1962b, 1970) develops Klein's idea of the epistemophilic impulse and Isaacs' idea that phantasy (unconscious thinking) is inherently knowledge-seeking into an idea that the human need to know the truth of one's experience is the primary impetus for thinking. A "sense of reality matters to the individual in the way that food, drink, air and excretion of waste products matter" (Bion, 1962a, p. 42). Unconscious thinking ("phantasy activity," in Isaacs' terms; "dreaming," in Bion's terms) is inherently directed toward bringing reality to bear on the process of coming to terms with one's emotional problems: "without [unconscious] phantasies and without dreams, you have not the means with which to think out your problems" (Bion, 1967, p. 25). Here, Bion makes explicit the idea that phantasying (unconscious thinking) underlies the psychological capacity to cope with one's emotional problems.

In sum, phantasying – from the vantage point of human psychology colored by epistemophilic (truth-seeking) needs – is not simply an effort to manage the tension of excess sexual and destructive impulses; in addition, phantasying is a form of thinking aimed at coming to understandings necessary for solving the emotional problems generated in response to lived emotional experience. This conception of unconscious phantasy activity is a highly "personal" theory of psychological development in that phantasying is seen as an attempt to get to know the truth of one's experience, an activity that involves developing personal, idiosyncratic ways of being curious, different sorts of getting to know, forms of doing something with what one is learning, and individual ways of using what one is coming to understand in the process of becoming who one is.

Isaacs' and Fairbairn's differing conceptions of phantasy

I find that Isaacs' conception of phantasy is clarified by comparing it with Fairbairn's (see Chapter 4 for a discussion of Fairbairn's work). The term "object relations theory" is commonly used in a way that encompasses both Klein's and Fairbairn's work. It seems to me that to do so conflates radically different conceptions of the internal object world and of the role of phantasy in that "inner world." Fairbairn (1943a) responded to Isaacs' paper in a letter read at the Second Discussion Meeting:

I cannot refrain from voicing the opinion that the explanatory concept of 'phantasy' has now been rendered obsolete by the concepts of 'psychical reality' and 'internal objects', which the work of Mrs Klein and her followers has done so much to develop; and in my opinion the time is now ripe for us to replace the concept of 'phantasy' by a concept of 'inner reality' peopled by the ego and its internal objects. These internal objects should be regarded as having an organized structure, an identity of their own, an endopsychic existence, and an activity [a capacity for thinking and feeling] as real within the inner world as those of any objects in the outer world. To attribute such features to internal objects may at first seem startling to some; but, after all, they are

51

only features which Freud has already attributed to the superego [in "Mourning and melancholia,' Freud, 1917a]. What has now emerged is simply that the superego is not the only internal object [i.e. split-off portion of the ego].

(Fairbairn, 1943a, pp. 359–360)

For Fairbairn, the internal object world is not a world constituted by phantasy ("which is an ideational process" [Fairbairn, 1943a, p. 359]). Internal objects are not ideas – they are split-off parts of the ego with which the internal world is "peopled" (a striking word choice on Fairbairn's part). Internal object relationships are actual interpersonal relationships between split-off and repressed sub-organizations of the self (ego) (Fairbairn, 1944) (see Ogden, 1983, and Chapter 4 for discussions of Fairbairn's conception of internal object relationships). These relationships are not phantasied relationships, they are "as real within the inner world as those of any objects in the outer world" (Fairbairn, 1943a, p. 359). Fairbairn, I believe, would say that people in "the outer world" do not phantasize their object relationships, they engage in them and experience them – which is also the case for the objects that "people" the unconscious inner world. "The concept of 'phantasy' is purely functional" (Fairbairn, 1943a, p. 360), that is, phantasying is an ego function: an activity of the main body of the ego/self (which Fairbairn [1944] calls the central ego) and its split-off and repressed sub-organizations. I would put the central difference between Isaacs and Fairbairn regarding phantasy and internal objects in the following terms: *For Isaacs, internal objects are the product of phantasying; for Fairbairn, phantasying is the product of internal objects (i.e. internal objects are the thinkers doing the unconscious thinking).*

Fairbairn and Isaacs differ in their understanding of phantasy in another important respect. Though Isaacs broadens the concept of phantasy to include not simply giving mental representation to instinctual impulses, but also giving mental representation to other types of experience, there remains in her work a strong emphasis on instinct as the principal source (beginning in earliest infancy) of unconscious desires, impulses, feeling states, and ways of organizing and understanding one's experience in the internal and external world. By contrast, for Fairbairn (1944), instinct-driven phantasying is not the principal source of the infant's response to lived experience with the mother (and the rest of external reality); rather, the infant's first encounter with the world is his response to the *real* mother (who is inevitably both a satisfactory and an unsatisfactory object). The infant's experience of emotional deprivation is a real experience, not a phantasy (for even the best of mothers sometimes misreads her infant, at other times withdraws emotionally, and at still other times exhausts her capacity to meet her infant's needs).

Isaacs' (1943b) reply to Fairbairn at the Discussion Meetings was terse and dismissive:

> Dr. Fairbairn, to my mind, overemphasizes and distorts certain parts of Mrs Klein's theories to the point of caricature. He over-substantifies internal objects and makes them far too independent, leaving wishes and feelings and the id generally out of account . . . Dr. Fairbairn's position is not to be taken as representing Mrs Klein's work or conclusions.
>
> (p. 458)

Isaacs' response to Fairbairn fails to address the theoretical problem that Fairbairn is pointing out: if the inner world is a metaphorical world constituted by phantasy, is the ego doing the phantasying? Or is it the id? Or is the distinction between ego and id no longer viable? Is Freud's structural model a model of psychic structure that is inconsistent with Klein's and Isaacs' theories, which hold as their principal metaphor the idea of an "inner world" of internal objects that interact with one another?

It may be that Isaacs gave Fairbairn's response further thought after the Controversial Discussions and after the publication of his paper, "Endopsychic structure considered in terms of object-relationships" (1944). Isaacs added a chapter note to the 1952 version of her paper in which she quotes Freud's comment that "one must not take the difference between ego and id in too hard-and-fast a sense" (Freud, 1923, quoted in Isaacs, 1952, p. 120). Perhaps this represents a movement on Isaacs' part in the direction of Fairbairn's idea that the id and ego are a single entity – the subject impelled by his needs and desires. If one adopts this position, the structural model collapses into a real internal object relationship between two unconscious sub-organizations of the self: the ego and a split-off part of the ego (the superego). The movement from Freud's structural model to a model of internal object relationships structured by phantasy seems to me to be a necessary implication of Isaacs' and Klein's work, but it is an implication that Isaacs seems to actively resist, perhaps for reasons having to do with the psychoanalytic politics of her time.

Concluding comments

Isaacs' conception of phantasy served, and still serves, as a transition from the "Freud–Klein era" of psychoanalysis in which emphasis is placed on the meaning of thoughts (*what* we think) to the "Winnicott– Bion era" in which emphasis is placed on *the way* we think. Isaacs had one foot in each of these eras. The principal importance of Isaacs' paper, it seems to me, is to be found in her idea that phantasy is the process that creates meaning, and is the form in which all meanings – including feelings, defense "mechanisms," impulses, bodily experiences, and so on – exist in unconscious mental life. In addition to this fundamental way of re-conceiving human "inner life," I find that there are in Isaacs' work other important implications for a revised theory of thinking that are left to the reader to develop. My own extensions of Isaacs' ideas include (1) the idea that phantasying generates not only unconscious psychic content, but also constitutes the entirety of unconscious thinking; (2) the notion that transference is a form of phantasying that serves as a way of thinking *for the first time* (in relation to the analyst) emotional events that occurred in the past, but were too disturbing to be experienced at the time they occurred; and (3) the idea that a principal aim and function of phantasy is that of fulfilling the human need to understand the truth of one's experience.

4

Why read Fairbairn?

I have found that Fairbairn develops a model of the mind that incorporates into its very structure a conceptualization of early psychic development that is not found in the writing of any other major twentieth-century analytic theorist. Fairbairn replaces Freud's (1923) structural model/metaphor of the mind with a model/metaphor in which the mind is conceived of as an "inner world" (Fairbairn, 1943b, p. 67) in which split-off and repressed parts of the self enter into stable, yet potentially alterable, object relationships with one another. The "cast of characters" (that is, sub-organizations of the personality) constituting Fairbairn's internal object world is larger than the triumvirate of Freud's structural model and provides what I find to be a richer set of metaphors with which to understand (1) certain types of human dilemmas, particularly those based on the fear that one's love is destructive; and (2) the central role played by feelings of resentment, contempt, disillusionment and addictive "love" in structuring the unconscious mind.

To my mind, Fairbairn's theory of internal object relations constitutes one of the most important contributions to the development of analytic theory in its first century. Yet, judging from the scarcity of references to his work in the analytic literature, particularly in North American and Latin American writing, his theoretical ideas (for example, ideas that he introduced in his 1940, 1941, 1943b and 1944 papers) and his clinical thinking (which he presented in his 1956 and 1958 papers) have attracted far less interest and study than have other major twentieth-century analytic theorists such as Klein, Winnicott and Bion. In part this is due to the fact that Fairbairn worked in isolation in Edinburgh. He had little opportunity for personal involvement or intellectual exchange with colleagues at the Institute of

Psychoanalysis in London whose members, in his era, included Balint, Bion, Anna Freud, Heimann, Klein, Milner, Rosenfeld, Segal, and Winnicott (Sutherland, 1989). Consequently, exposure to his work, even for his contemporaries, was almost entirely through his writing.

Fairbairn's relatively marginal place in psychoanalysis today also derives, I believe, from the fact that the reader who undertakes the study of Fairbairn finds himself confronted by a dense prose style, a highly abstract form of theorizing and a set of unfamiliar theoretical terms (for example, dynamic structure, endopsychic structure, central ego, internal saboteur, libidinal ego, exciting object, rejecting object, and so on) that have not been adopted by subsequent analytic theorists. Though Fairbairn's terminology is little used currently, his ideas have had considerable impact on the thinking of leading analytic theorists including Greenberg and Mitchell (1983), Grotstein (1994), Guntrip (1968), Kernberg (1980), Klein (1946), Kohut (1971), Modell (1968), Rinsley (1977), Scharff and Scharff (1994), Sutherland (1989) and Symington (1986). It is beyond the scope of this paper to explore the ways in which these authors have critiqued, modified and extended Fairbairn's thinking.

In this paper, it is not my intention simply to offer an explication and clarification of Fairbairn's thinking; rather, in the process of looking closely at Fairbairn's work (particularly his papers "Schizoid factors in the personality" [1940] and "Endopsychic structure considered in terms of object-relationships" [1944]), I develop what I believe to be several important implications and extensions of his thinking. I attempt to make something of my own with Fairbairn's writings, in part by means of a close reading of his texts, and in part by clinically illustrating how Fairbairn's ideas have shaped, and evolved in, my own analytic work.

Elements of Fairbairn's revision of psychoanalytic theory

For Fairbairn, the most difficult and most psychically formative psychological problem that the infant or child faces is the dilemma that arises when he experiences his mother (upon whom he is utterly dependent) as both loving and accepting of his love, and unloving and rejecting of his love. Fairbairn's writing contains a critical ambiguity concerning this core human dilemma. The language that Fairbairn uses repeatedly raises in the reader's mind the questions: Is every infant traumatized by experiences of deficits in his mother's love for him?

Or does the infant misinterpret inevitable (and necessary) frustrations as manifestations of his mother's failure to love him? There is ample evidence in Fairbairn's work to support both conclusions. For instance, in support of the idea that the infant responds to privation as if it were willful rejection on the part of the mother, Fairbairn writes:

> Here it must be pointed out that what presents itself to him [the infant or child] from a strictly conative standpoint as *frustration* at the hands of his mother presents itself to him in a very different light from a strictly affective standpoint. From the latter standpoint, what he experiences is a sense of lack of love, and indeed emotional *rejection* on his mother's part.
>
> (Fairbairn, 1944, pp. 112–113)

At the same time, there is a persistent logic in Fairbairn's work that supports the idea that every infant realistically perceives the limits of his mother's capacity to love him and that this realistic perception is "traumatic" (Fairbairn, 1944, p. 110) for the infant or child. This logic goes as follows: (1) "[E]verybody without exception must be regarded as schizoid" (Fairbairn, 1940, p. 7), that is, everyone evidences pathological splitting of the self; individuals differ from one another only in the severity of their schizoid pathology; (2) Schizoid psychopathology has its origins in an "unsatisfactory" (Fairbairn, 1940, p. 13) relationship with the mother, i. e. there is a "failure on the part of the mother to convince the child that she really loves him as a person" (p. 13); (3) Since everyone is schizoid, and the schizoid condition derives from maternal failure to convince the infant of her love, it follows that every infant experiences traumatizing maternal failure to love. But the language used in this logical sequence leaves open an important ambiguity. Does "failure on the part of the mother to convince the child that she really loves him as a person" (Fairbairn, 1940, p. 13) reflect the mother's failure to be convincing, or does it reflect the child's failure/inability to be convinced, that is, the child's inability to accept love? The clause "failure on the part of the mother," to my ear, leans in the direction of the former interpretation, but by no means rules out the latter. Overall, in Fairbairn's work, ambiguity of language in this connection serves to convey what I believe to be Fairbairn's view that every infant or child accurately perceives the limits of the mother's ability to love him; and, at the same time, every infant or child misinterprets inevitable privations as the mother's lack of love for him. From this vantage point, Fairbairn's conception of early psychic development is a trauma theory in which the infant, to varying degrees, is traumatized by his realistic perception that he is fully dependent on a mother whose capacity to love him has passed its breaking point. (To my mind, Fairbairn's and Klein's object relations theories are complementary, and this complementarity creates the opportunity for us, as analysts, to think/see with "binocular vision" [Bion, 1962a, p. 86]. Fairbairn believes in the primacy of external reality and the secondary role of unconscious phantasy, while Klein believes in the primary role of unconscious phantasy and the secondary effect of external reality. [Space does not allow for an elaboration of the comparison of Fairbairn's and Klein's object relations theories.])

Fairbairn (1944) states that the infant's subjective sense that his mother, upon whom he depends utterly, is unable to love him generates "an affective experience which is singularly devastating" (p. 113). For an older child, the experience of loving the mother who is experienced as unloving and unaccepting of his love is one of "intense humiliation" (p. 113). "At a somewhat deeper level (or at an earlier stage) the experience is one of shame over the display of needs which are disregarded or belittled" (p. 113). The child "feels reduced to a state of worthlessness, destitution or beggardom" (p. 113). "At the same time his sense of badness [for demanding too much] is further complicated by the sense of utter impotence" (p. 113).

But, the pain of the feelings of shame, worthlessness, beggardom, badness and impotence is not the most catastrophic consequence of the infant's dependence on a mother whom he experiences as unloving and unaccepting of his love. Even more devastating is the threat to the infant's very existence that is posed by that relationship:

> At a still deeper level (or at a still earlier stage) the child's experience is one of, so to speak, exploding ineffectively and being completely emptied of libido. It is thus an experience of disintegration and of imminent psychical death . . . [In being] threatened with loss of his libido [love] (which for him constitutes his own goodness) . . . [he is threatened by the loss of what] constitutes himself.
>
> (Fairbairn, 1944, p. 113)

In other words, a universal part of earliest post-natal human existence is the terrifying experience of imminent loss of one's self, loss of one's life. What is more, the infant or child feels that the reason for his mother's apparent lack of love towards him is that he has destroyed her affection and made it disappear. At the same time he feels that the reason for her apparent refusal to accept his love is that his own love is destructive and bad.

(Fairbairn, 1940, p. 25)

The infant persists in his love of "bad objects" (Fairbairn, 1943b, p. 67) because bad objects are better than no objects at all: "he [the infant or child] *needs* them [maternal objects] . . . he cannot do without them" (Fairbairn, 1943b, p. 67). Hence, the infant cannot abandon his attempts to reestablish a loving tie to the unloving and unaccepting mother. The infant, in clinging to the unloving mother, is attempting to undo the imagined toxic effects of his own love. But if the infant persists too long in attempting to wring love from the unloving mother, he will suffer "disintegration and . . . imminent psychical death" (Fairbairn, 1944, p. 113).

From this vantage point, the most important (life-sustaining) task faced by the infant is not simply that of establishing and maintaining a loving tie with the mother who is capable of giving and receiving love. At least as important to the psychical survival of the infant is his capacity to extricate himself from his futile efforts to wring love from the external object mother who is experienced as unloving. The infant achieves this life-saving psychological maneuver by developing an internal object world (an aspect of mind) in which the relationship with the external unloving mother is transformed into an internal object relationship.

The infant incorporates the breast in order to control it: "*relationships with internalized objects,* [are relationships] *to which the individual is compelled to turn in default of a satisfactory relationship with objects in the outer world*" (Fairbairn, 1941, p. 40). In replacing a real external object relationship with an internal one, the infant staunches the hemorrhaging of libido (his "nascent love" [Fairbairn, 1944, p. 113]) into an emotional vacuum (the mother who, for real and imagined reasons, is experienced as unloving). By creating an internal object relationship with the unloving mother, the infant directs his nascent object love toward an internal object, an object that is a part of himself. (Every aspect of one's mind – including all of the "internalized figures" constituting one's internal object world – is necessarily an aspect of oneself.)

For Fairbairn, an internal object relationship constitutes a real relationship between aspects of the ego. The meaning of the term *ego*, as

Fairbairn uses it, is better conveyed by the term *self* since all the split-off "parts" of "the ego" are sub-organizations of the self. Fairbairn (1943b) drops the term *id* from his lexicon because he views one's impulses and passions as integral parts of the ego/self. In discussing Fairbairn's ideas, I will use the terms *ego* and *self* interchangeably. Fairbairn (1943b, 1944) reminds the reader again and again that to conceive of internal object relationships as relationships between a pair of split-off parts of the ego is to do nothing more than to elaborate on Freud's (1917a) conception of the creation of the "critical agency" (p. 248) (later to be called the superego). In "Mourning and melancholia," Freud (1917a) describes the process by which two parts of the ego are split off from the main body of the ego (the "I") and enter into an unconscious relationship with one another. In melancholia, a part of the self (which harbors feelings of impotent rage toward the abandoning object) enters into a stable internal object relationship with another split-off part of the ego (which is identified with the abandoning object). In this way, an actual unconscious object relationship between different aspects of the self is established and maintained. The upshot of this splitting of the ego, in Freud's view, is an unconscious feeling that one has not lost the object since the abandoning object has been replaced by a part of oneself. Thus, Fairbairn's theory of internal object relationships represents both an elaboration of Freud's thinking (see Chapter 2 for a discussion of the origins of object relations theory in "Mourning and melancholia") and a radical departure from it (in his understanding of endopsychic structure and the nature of internal object relationships).

Having discussed the infant's replacement of unsatisfactory external object relationships with internal ones, I will now turn to Fairbairn's conception of the internal object world ("the basic endopsychic situation" [Fairbairn, 1944, p. 106]) that results from internalization of the unsatisfactory relationship with the mother.

To understand Fairbairn's conception of the development of the psyche it is necessary to understand his notion of "endopsychic structure" (Fairbairn, 1944, p. 120). In brief, an endopsychic structure is a sub-organization of the self (split off from the main "body" of the ego/self). For Fairbairn, all unconscious endopsychic structures are split-off parts of the ego/self; and yet, he misleadingly uses the term *internal objects* to refer to these split-off parts of the self, which are more accurately termed *internal subjects*. Fairbairn believes that it is erroneous to separate "endopsychic structures" (parts of the self capable of thinking, feeling, remembering and responding in their own distinctive ways) from "psychic dynamism" (our impulses, wishes, needs and desires). Fairbairn (1943b, 1944) differs in this regard with Freud and Klein in that he believes that it is inaccurate to posit an aspect of the self (the ego/I) that is devoid of impulses, wishes and desires: What is a self devoid of desires and impulses? Similarly, the idea of desire or impulse divorced from the self/ego/I that is desiring or feels impelled, is, for Fairbairn, "utterly meaningless" (Fairbairn, 1944, p. 95): "'impulses' are inseparable from an ego structure with a definite pattern" (Fairbairn, 1944, p. 90). Note that Fairbairn specifies that the "ego structure" has "a definite pattern." This idea reflects his view that each "ego structure" (that is, each aspect of the self) has its own unique organization that defines the way it experiences and responds to its perceptions, needs and desires. Feeling slighted, for example, is a different experience for each ego structure (i.e. each quasi-autonomous aspect of the self) and elicits from each ego structure qualitatively different emotional responses (for example, feelings of resentment, contempt, vindictiveness and so on).

In an effort to simplify and thereby gain some control over the internalized relationship with the unloving mother, the infant engages in a "divide et impera" (Fairbairn, 1944, p. 112) maneuver. The infant divides the unloving (internal object) mother into two parts: the tantalizing mother and the rejecting mother. Fairbairn does not explain how he has arrived at the idea that the infant divides his experience of the unloving mother into tantalizing and rejecting parts. (Why not postulate jealous and murderous parts, or poisonous and devouring parts?) As we do with Freud's even bolder proposal that all human motivations are derived from the sexual instinct and the ego (or survival) instinct (later replaced by the death instinct), we must suspend judgment while we examine the theoretical and clinical consequences of the author's hypothesis.

Fairbairn (1944) proposes that an aspect of the infant's personality feels powerfully, uncontrollably attached to the alluring aspect of the internal object mother, while another aspect of the infant's personality feels hopelessly attached to the rejecting aspect of the internal object mother. Both parts of the infant's psyche – the part emotionally bound to the alluring mother and the part bound to the rejecting mother – are "split off" (Fairbairn, 1944, p. 112) from the healthy main body of the ego (which Fairbairn terms the *central ego*). At the same time, aspects of the infant's personality that are thoroughly identified with the alluring and with the rejecting aspects of the mother are also split off from the central ego. Thus, two repressed internal object relationships (made up of four split-off parts of the central ego) are created: (1) the relationship of the tantalized self (termed by Fairbairn the *libidinal ego*) and the tantalizing self-identified-with-the-object (the exciting object); and (2) the relationship of the rejected self (the internal saboteur) and the rejecting self-identified-with-the-object (the rejecting object). These two sets of internal object relationships are angrily rejected (that is, repressed) by the central ego because the healthy aspect of the infant's personality (the central ego) feels intense anger at the unloving internal object mother.

The exciting object and the rejecting object are no less parts of the self than are the libidinal ego and the internal saboteur. The exciting and rejecting internal "objects" have a not-me feel to them because they are parts of the self that are thoroughly identified with the unloving mother in her exciting and rejecting qualities (see Ogden, 1983, for a discussion of the concept of internal objects and internal object relations).

Fairbairn (1944, 1963) believes that the internalization of the unsatisfactory object is a defensive measure carried out in an effort to control the unsatisfactory object. But, to my mind, the illusory control that the child achieves by means of this internalization only in part accounts for the immense psychic power of the internal object world to remain a "closed system of internal reality" (Fairbairn, 1958, p. 385), that is, to maintain its isolation from the real world. Despite the fact that split-off and repressed aspects of the ego (the internal saboteur and libidinal ego) feel intense resentment toward, and feelings of being callously spurned by, the unloving and unaccepting object, Fairbairn (1944) states that the ties between these split-off parts of the self and the internalized unloving object are libidinal in nature.

The libidinal nature of these ties suggests that aspects of the individual (the internal saboteur and the libidinal ego) have by no means given up on the potential of the unsatisfactory object to give and receive love. It seems to me that a libidinal tie to an internal object toward whom one feels anger, resentment, and the like necessarily involves an (unconscious) wish/need to use what control one feels one has to change the unloving and unaccepting (internal) object into a loving and accepting one.

From this vantage point, I view the libidinal ego and the internal saboteur as aspects of self that are intent on transforming the exciting object and the rejecting object into loving objects. Moreover, it seems to me, by extension of Fairbairn's thinking, that *the infant's effort to transform unsatisfactory objects into satisfactory objects – thus reversing the imagined toxic effect on the mother of the infant's love – is the single most important motivation sustaining the structure of the internal object world.* And that structure, when externalized, underlies all pathological object relationships.

The "emotional life" of Fairbairn's internal objects

Fairbairn (1944, p. 105) provides a diagram depicting the relationships among the psychic structures that I have just described (see *Figure 1*). It has been my experience in reading and teaching Fairbairn that a familiarity with this diagram is useful in one's efforts to grasp the nature of the internal object world as Fairbairn conceives it. Since

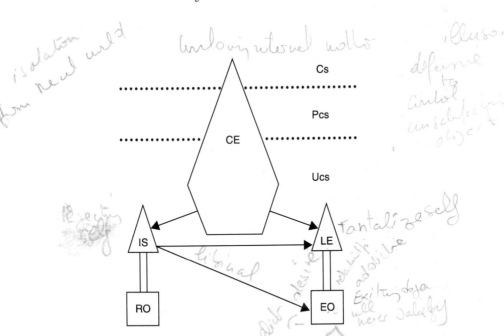

Figure 1 Relationships among the psychic structures. Adapted from Fairbairn, 1944, p. 105. Permission kindly granted by Routledge & Kegan Paul.
Key: CE, Central Ego; IS, Internal Saboteur; LE, Libidinal Ego; RO, Rejecting Object; EO, Exciting Object; Cs, Conscious; Pcs, Preconscious; Ucs, Unconscious; →, Aggression; | |, Libido

63

the diagram necessarily has a mechanical, non-human quality to it, in what follows I try to convey what I believe to be the nature of the "emotional life" of each of the internal objects constituting Fairbairn's internal object world.

Addictive love (the bond between the libidinal ego and the exciting object)

As I understand Fairbairn's theory of internal object relationships, all the love and hate that tie internal objects to one another is inherently pathological because it is derived entirely from the pathological tie of the infant to the unreachable mother, that is, to the mother who is felt to be incapable of giving and receiving love. The relationship between the libidinal ego and the exciting object is one of addictive "love" on the part of the libidinal ego, and of desperate need on the part of the exciting object to elicit desire from the libidinal ego (which desire the exciting object will never satisfy).

When I imagine the libidinal ego and the exciting object as characters in an internal drama, I often think of a patient with whom I worked many years ago in twice-weekly face-to-face psychotherapy. The patient, Mr. C, was a man in his early thirties, with cerebral palsy, who was desperately in love with Ms. Z, a "beautiful" woman friend (who did not have cerebral palsy or any other physical impairment). In the course of the years of this "friendship," the patient's advances became more insistent and beseeching. This eventually led Ms. Z to end the relationship altogether. Mr. C, who found it difficult to articulate words under the best of circumstances, would bellow in pain during our sessions as he tried to talk about how much he loved Ms. Z.

Mr. C insisted that Ms. Z must love him because she enjoyed his sense of humor and had invited him to two parties at her apartment. Although I only knew Ms. Z from my experience with Mr. C (including my transference–countertransference experience), I suspected that Ms. Z was drawn to Mr. C in an unconscious pathological way. I based this suspicion, in part, on the fact that in my work with Mr. C, I regularly had the wish not only to soothe him, but also to "cure" him of his cerebral palsy. I came to see the latter wish as a reflection of my own inability to appreciate and accept him as he was, and, instead, to turn to magical solutions. To have acted on these feelings, for example, by speaking to Mr. C in a way that implicitly promised "cure" would have been to encourage the patient to become utterly dependent on me for continued magical evasion of reality. Under such circumstances, there would have been no opportunity for Mr. C to grow and to achieve genuine maturity and independence. It seems to me that the outcome of the analytic work depended upon my ability to recognize, think about, and come to terms with my own needs to keep Mr. C endlessly dependent on me.

To my mind, Mr. C's "love relationship" with Ms. Z (and with me in the aspect of the transference–countertransference that involved my unconscious wish to "cure" him) was an expression of a pathological mutual dependence. In Fairbairn's terms, this emotional situation might be thought of as the tie between the libidinal ego and the exciting object. Such relationships involve psychic bondage in which the participants are each jailer and jailed, stalker and stalked. (I will further discuss my work with Mr. C later in this chapter when I address the subject of psychological growth.)

Bonds of resentment (the tie between the internal saboteur and the rejecting object)

The relationship between the internal saboteur and the rejecting object derives from the infant's love of his mother despite (and because of) her rejection of him. The nature of the pathological love that binds together the internal saboteur and the rejecting object is a bond not of hate, but of a pathological love that is experienced as bitter "resentment" (Fairbairn, 1944, p. 115). Neither the rejecting object nor the internal saboteur is willing or able to think about, much less relinquish, that tie. In fact, there is no desire on the part of either to change anything about their mutual dependence. The power of that bond is impossible to overestimate. The rejecting object and the internal saboteur are determined to nurse their feelings of having been deeply wronged, cheated, humiliated, betrayed, exploited, treated unfairly, discriminated against, and so on. The mistreatment at the hands of the other is felt to be unforgivable. An apology is forever expected by each, but never offered by either. Nothing is more important to the internal saboteur (the rejected self) than coercing the rejecting object into recognizing the incalculable pain that he or she has caused.

From the point of view of the rejecting object (the split-off aspect of the self thoroughly identified with the rejecting mother), the experience of this form of pathological love involves the conviction that the internal saboteur is greedy, insatiable, thin-skinned, ungrateful, unwilling to be reasonable, unable to let go of a grudge, and so on. But despite the burdensomeness of the ceaseless complaining and self-righteous outrage of the internal saboteur, the rejecting object is both unwilling and unable to give up the relationship, that is, to extricate itself from the mutual pathological dependence. The life, the determination, the very reason for being of the rejecting object (as a part of the self) is derived from its tie to the internal saboteur. The rejecting object is an empty shell, a lost and forgotten part of the past, in the absence of the obsession on the part of the internal saboteur to wring love, remorse and magical reparation from it. This internal object relationship (like the relationship of the libidinal ego and the exciting object) is a relationship in which the jailer is a prisoner of the jailed, and the jailed a prisoner of the jailer. Outside of the terms of their pathological, mutually dependent "love," neither would hold meaning for the other or for itself (much less for any other part of the self). In the absence of one, the other would become a mere remnant of a once powerful pair of deities that reigned in a religion no longer practised.

A particular clinical experience of group dynamics comes to mind in connection with the power of the bond between the internal saboteur and the rejecting object. (While Fairbairn [1944] believed that his understanding of the psyche "provides a more satisfactory basis than does any other type of psychology for the explanation of group phenomena" [p. 128], he did not develop or clinically illustrate this idea in any of his writings.) I was asked by the chairperson of a social service agency to serve as a consultant to the psychotherapy division of the agency. The members of the staff of the psychotherapy division were in constant conflict with one another and with the rest of the agency. The director of the psychotherapy division, a psychiatrist in his early fifties, oversaw a staff of three male psychiatrists and six female psychologists and social workers, all in their thirties and forties. The director showed consistent favoritism toward the male psychiatrists, not only in his praise of their ideas, but also in appointing them to leadership positions (which paid higher salaries). The women therapists, most of whom had worked in this agency for many years, made no secret of their discontent with the director.

In the course of speaking in confidence with individual members of the staff, I was struck by the fact that while each of the female psychotherapists expressed intense anger and bitterness about the way she was being treated by the director, they all felt that they had no choice but to remain working at the clinic. They told me that psychiatric services at the other agencies and hospitals in the area were being shut down, so they had no choice but to stay. But none had interviewed at other hospitals or social service agencies. In my conversations with the director of the division, he spoke to me as a fellow psychiatrist whom he believed would understand the inevitable difficulty involved in working with "non-medical" female psychotherapists who invariably become ensnarled in "oedipal attachments and rivalries" with one another and with the "medical" group leader.

My consultation to the clinic was ended abruptly after three months when the city's funding for all mental health services was cut sharply and the psychotherapy division of this clinic was shut down. One of the female staff members, whom I later met by chance at a lecture, told me, "On looking back on it, I feel as if I was living as a child in a psychotic family. I couldn't imagine leaving and finding other work. It felt as if I would end up living in a cardboard box if I were to leave. My whole world had shrunk to the size of that clinic. If the clinic hadn't closed, I'm certain I would still be working there." She described the former director of the psychotherapy division as "a very limited person who hates women and gets pleasure out of humiliating them in a way that he feels no need to hide." "But," she added, "the really frightening thing for me is that I couldn't leave. The situation was not only bad at work, I couldn't stop thinking about it at night, over the weekends, or even when I was on vacation. It was as if I was infected by the situation."

It seems to me that all of the participants in this drama felt and behaved as if their lives depended on the perpetuation of the tie between the tormentor and the aggrieved. The director, the three psychiatrists (who said they felt "caught in the middle," but did nothing to address the patent unfairness), and the female staff all felt wronged. No one seemed to recognize the ways in which he or she actively and passively provoked feelings of anger, helplessness, outrage and resentment in the others. In retrospect, it seems to me that what I was witnessing might be thought of as a rather intense form of the bond of mutual dependence tying the internal saboteur and the rejecting object to one another.

Bonds of contempt (the relationship of the internal saboteur to the libidinal ego and the exciting object)

For me, one of Fairbairn's most original and most significant contributions to psychoanalysis is the understanding of human nature that emerges from his conception of the relationship between the internal saboteur and the libidinal ego, and between the internal saboteur and the exciting object. The internal saboteur, filled with self-hatred for its own "dependence dictated by . . . [infantile] need" (Fairbairn, 1944, p. 115), turns on the libidinal ego, and in so doing, turns on itself at one remove (since every internal object – every endopsychic structure – is a subdivision of a subject who is one person). The internal saboteur disdainfully, contemptuously attacks the libidinal ego as a pathetic wretch, a sap, a sucker for the way it continually humiliates itself in begging for the love of the exciting object: You [the libidinal ego] never learn your lesson. You get kicked in the face [by the exciting object] and drag yourself to your feet as if nothing has happened only to get kicked and knocked down again. How can you be so stupid as to not see what is plain as day? She [the exciting object] toys with you, leads you on, and then dumps you every time. And yet you keep going back for more. You disgust me.

It seems to me that from this perspective – the perspective of the internal saboteur – we are better able to understand the sense in which Fairbairn uses the term *libidinal ego* to name the aspect of self that is tied by bonds of addictive love to the exciting object. Libido, in this context, and in the internal object world in general, is synonymous with narcissistic libido (narcissistic love). All internal objects (more accurately, internal subjects) are split-off parts of the central ego/self, and therefore the relationships among them are relationships that are exclusively relationships with oneself. Thus, the libidinal ego is "loving," but only loving of itself (in the form of the exciting object).

Closely tied to the attack of the internal saboteur on the libidinal ego is the attack of the internal saboteur on the object of that narcissistic love, the exciting object. The internal saboteur views the exciting object as a malicious tease, a seductress, a bundle of empty promises: You [the exciting object] don't fool me. You may be able to make a fool of him [the libidinal ego], but I know your type, I've heard your lies, I've seen your depraved imitations of love. You're a parasite; you take, but you don't know what it means to give. You prey on the gullible, on children.

At first blush, the internal saboteur deserves its name: it demeans and shames the libidinal ego for its infantile longings, and attacks the exciting object for its endless appetite for tantalizing, seducing, deceiving and humiliating. But the contempt and disdain that the internal saboteur feels toward the libidinal ego and the exciting object are born of its feelings of self-hatred, impotence and shame concerning its own naive, self-deluding, infantile pursuit of the love of the rejecting object (for example, in the clinical example presented earlier, the futile pursuit of the love of the director by the female members of the therapy staff). I believe that implicit in Fairbairn's rendering of the structure of the internal object world is the idea that the fury and contempt that the internal saboteur heaps upon the libidinal ego and the exciting object stem from a glimmer of recognition of the shame and humiliation it feels about its own absolute dependence on, and loyalty to, the rejecting (internal object) mother.

Attacks by the internal saboteur on the libidinal ego and the exciting object may take a broad range of forms in the analytic situation. In my work with Ms. T, an analysand I saw over a period of many years in a five-session-per-week analysis, I could do nothing right. If I spoke, I was "missing the point"; if I was quiet, I was "being a stereotypic analyst," spewing pronouncements from behind the couch; if I was punctual, I was "being obsessional"; if I was a minute late, I was "dreading" seeing her. In a session with this patient in the fourth year of analysis, an image came to my mind of a homeless man sitting on the curb near a traffic light. It seemed that he had given up on begging, and that it would not be long before he died. Profoundly disturbed by this image, I began to become aware of my own feeling that for a number of months I had given up on ever being seen by the patient for who I was, and, in return, I had given up on trying to be an analyst to her. It was not simply that I had made mistakes; the situation felt to me to be far worse than that: I, myself, was the mistake. My very being was wrong for her.

An integral part of my effort to make therapeutic use of the feeling state that I was beginning to recognize and put into words for myself involved thinking of myself as having experienced something like the patient's feeling that her very way of being was wrong (a far worse problem than feeling that she had made a great many serious errors). (Fairbairn [1944] notes that in the world of unconscious internal object relationships, feeling guilty about one's failures and misdeeds is far preferable to feeling "unconditionally, i.e. libidinally bad" [p. 93]. To feel unconditionally bad is to feel that one's love is bad.) I eventually said to Ms. T, "For a long time, you have been telling me that I simply cannot understand you and that virtually everything I say confirms that. I don't think you've been any harsher with me than you are with yourself. In fact, I think that your attacks on yourself are far more violent than your attacks on me. I think that you feel not only that everything you do is wrong, you firmly believe that your very existence is wrong and that the only thing you can do to remedy that situation is to become another person. Of course, if you were to succeed in doing so, you would be dead: worse than that, you would never have existed."

Ms. T responded immediately by saying that I was being very wordy. As she said this, I felt deflated and realized that despite years of experience with this patient, I had actually expected that this time she would at least consider what I had said. I told this to the patient and after a few moments of silence, she said, "Please don't give up on me." In Fairbairn's terms, the patient, at least for this moment, had softened her intrapsychic attack on herself (the attack of the internal saboteur on the libidinal ego for its way of loving). She allowed herself not only to accept her dependence on me, but also to ask something of me (as a separate person) that she knew she could not provide for herself.

The relationship of the central ego to internal and external objects

Before ending the discussion of the emotional life of internal objects/ endopsychic structures, I will comment very briefly on Fairbairn's concept of the central ego. The central ego is the aspect of the psyche that Fairbairn fleshes out least. What Fairbairn (1944) does say is that the central ego is an endopsychic structure capable of thinking, feeling, responding, and so on. It constitutes the original healthy self of the newborn infant. From the outset, the central ego of the infant is capable of rudimentary self–object differentiation and of operating on the basis of the reality principle. But in response to a traumatizing experience with a mother whom the infant experiences as both loving and accepting of his love, and unloving and rejecting of his love, the infant splits off parts of the central ego and represses them in the form of the internal object relationships that I have described. Consequently, the central ego retains its original health, but is significantly depleted by the process of splitting off and "sending into exile" (repressing) parts of itself.

The central ego is the only part of the self that is able to engage in, and learn from, experience with external objects. Change in the unconscious internal object world is always mediated by the central ego (which sometimes acts in concert with external objects such as the analyst). Internal objects interact with the external world only in the form of narcissistic object relationships – that is, externalizations of internal object relationships (which are necessarily narcissistic in nature). The central ego includes no dynamically repressed (unsatisfactory) internal object relationships; rather, the central ego consists exclusively of good enough (as opposed to idealized) object relationships such as identifications with people whom one has loved and by whom one has felt loved, recognized and accepted. Such identifications underlie feelings that include a sense of internal security, as well as background feelings of solidity and integrity.

Psychological growth

In the final section of this paper, I will discuss some of the ways in which a person may be helped to grow psychologically. Fairbairn regards as "relatively immutable" (1944, p. 129) the "basic endopsychic situation," i.e. the constellations of split-off and repressed aspects of the central ego. For Fairbairn, the psychological changes that can be achieved through psychoanalysis primarily involve diminutions of the intensity of the feelings of resentment, addictive love, contempt, primitive dependence, disillusionment, and so on that bind the split-off, repressed sub-organizations of the self to one another. Specifically, healthy psychological change can be achieved by reducing to a minimum:

> (a) the attachment of the subsidiary egos [the internal saboteur and the libidinal ego] to their respective associated objects [the rejecting object and the exciting object], (b) the aggression of the central ego towards the subsidiary egos and their objects [which takes the form of repression of the two pairs of split-off parts of the self], and (c) the aggression of the internal saboteur towards the libidinal ego and its object [the exciting object].
>
> (Fairbairn, 1944, p. 130)

71

The density of the prose, the mechanical nature of the metaphors, the level of abstraction, the heavy reliance on his own technical terminology, together denude Fairbairn's statement of almost anything recognizable as human experience. I will offer an alternative way of speaking and thinking about how people grow psychologically that relies less on Fairbairn's explicitly stated ideas and more on ideas that I find to be implicit in his work. Though Fairbairn never puts it in this way, I believe that the most fundamental psychological principle underlying his conception of psychological growth is the idea that all psychological maturation involves the patient's genuine acceptance of himself and, by extension, acceptance of others. That acceptance is achieved by means of the work of coming to terms with the full range of aspects of oneself, including one's disturbing, infantile, split-off identifications with one's unloving, unaccepting mother. Psychological change of this sort creates the possibility of discovering a world of people and experiences that exists outside of oneself, a world in which it is possible to feel curious, surprised, delighted, disappointed, homesick, and so on. The world of thought, feeling and human relatedness that is opened by such self-acceptance is a world in which one feels no compulsion to transform the realities of one's human relationships into something other than what they are, that is, to change oneself or "the object" (who is now a whole and separate subject) into other people. It is also a world in which one can learn from one's experiences with other people because those experiences are no longer dominated by projections of static internal object relationships.

A particular analytic experience comes to mind in this regard. Mr. C, the patient with cerebral palsy whom I discussed earlier, had, as a child, been savaged by his mother. As I have described, in adult life he became possessed by a "love" for Ms. Z. Over a period of eight years, Ms. Z twice relocated to a different city; both times the patient followed. Again and again, she tried to make it clear to Mr. C that she liked him as a friend, but did not want a romantic relationship with him. He became increasingly desperate, angry and suicidal. From the outset of the analytic work, and frequently thereafter, the patient told me that he did not know why I "tolerated" him.

In our sessions, Mr. C would howl in pain as he spoke of the "unfairness" of Ms. Z's rejection of him. When upset, particularly when crying, the patient would lose muscular control of his mouth, which made it very difficult for him to speak. Frothy saliva gathered at the sides of his mouth and mucus dripped from his nose while tears ran down his cheeks. Being with Mr. C at these times was heart-breaking. I have only rarely felt in such an immediate, physical way that I was the mother of a baby in distress. Mr. C seemed to want me to help him present himself to Ms. Z in a way that would not frighten her and would help her understand how much he loved her and how much she loved him (if she would only admit it to herself). It was impossible not to hear in the patient's "plan" a wish that I transform Ms. Z (and, unconsciously, his mother and the aspect of me that only "tolerated" him) into people who were genuinely able to love him, accept him and value his love.

In retrospect, I believe that it was very important to the analytic experience that Mr. C experience for himself over a period of years the reality that I was not repulsed by him even when he bellowed in pain and could not control the release of tears, nasal mucus and saliva. It must have been apparent to Mr. C, though I never put it into words, that I loved him as I would one day love my own children in their infancy. For years, the patient had been too ashamed to tell me about some of the ways his mother had humiliated him as a child, for example, by repeatedly calling him "a repulsive, slobbering monster." He only gradually entrusted me with these deeply shamed aspects of himself.

I viewed Mr. C's accounts of his humiliating mother as a description not only of his external object mother, but, as importantly, a description of an aspect of himself that viewed himself as an object of contempt and which enlisted others (most prominently Ms. Z) to humiliate him. A humiliating connection with Ms. Z was unconsciously felt to be far better than no connection at all.

Several years into the work, Mr. C told me a dream: "Not much happened in the dream. I was myself with my cerebral palsy, washing my car and enjoying listening to music on the car radio that I had turned up loud." The dream was striking in a number of ways. It was the first time, in telling me a dream, that Mr. C specifically mentioned his cerebral palsy. Moreover, the way that he put it – "I was myself with my cerebral palsy" – conveyed a depth of recognition and an acceptance of himself that I had never before heard from him. How better could he have expressed a particular type of change in his relationship to himself – a psychological change that involved a loving self-recognition that contributed to freeing him from the need to perpetually attempt to wring love and acceptance from those internal and external objects who were least inclined to, or incapable of, loving him? In the dream, he was able to be a mother who took pleasure in bathing her baby (his car) while listening to and enjoying the music that was coming from inside the baby. This was not a dream of triumph; it was an ordinary dream of ordinary love: "nothing much happened."

I was deeply moved by the patient's telling me his dream. I said to him, "What a wonderful dream that was."

Some years later, Mr. C moved to another part of the country to take a high-level job in his field. He wrote to me periodically. In the last letter I received from him (about five years after we stopped working together), he told me that he had married a woman he loved, a woman who had cerebral palsy. They had recently had a healthy baby girl.

Mr. C, in the context of the developing relationship with me, was able to extricate himself from his addictive love of Ms. Z (a bond between the libidinal ego and the exciting object) while at the same time diminishing his compulsive engagement in forms of relatedness based on the bond between the debasing and the debased aspects of himself (the bond between the internal saboteur and the libidinal ego).

It seems to me that a key element of the therapeutic action of the work that Mr. C and I did together was the real (as opposed to the transferential) relationship between the two of us (for example, in my genuinely not feeling repulsed by the mucus, tears and saliva flowing from his nose, eyes and mouth as he bellowed in pain, and by my experiencing love for him of a sort that, later in my life, I would feel for my infant sons). Fairbairn, I think, would agree with this understanding and go a step further: "the really decisive [therapeutic] factor is the relationship of the patient to the analyst" (Fairbairn, 1958, p. 379). He elaborated on this idea a bit later in the same paper:

> *Psycho-analytical treatment resolves itself into a struggle on the part of the patient to press-gang his relationship with the analyst into the closed system of the inner world through the agency of transference, and a determination on the part of the analyst to effect a breach in this closed system and to provide conditions under which, in the setting of a therapeutic relationship, the patient may be induced to accept the open system of outer reality.*
>
> (p. 385)

Concluding comments

Psychological growth, for Fairbairn (as I read him), involves a form of acceptance of oneself that can be achieved only in the context of a real relationship with a relatively psychologically mature person. A relationship of this sort (including the analytic relationship) is the only possible exit from the solipsistic world of internal object relationships. Self-acceptance is a state of mind that marks the (never fully achieved) relinquishment of the life-consuming effort to transform unsatisfactory internal object relationships into satisfactory (that is, loving and accepting) ones. With psychological growth, one comes to know at depth that one's early experiences with one's unloving and unaccepting mother will never be other than what they were. It is a waste of life to devote oneself to the effort to transform oneself (and others) into the people one wishes one were (or wishes they were). In order to take part in experience in a world populated by people whom one has not invented, and from whom one may learn, the individual must first loosen the unconscious bonds of resentment, addictive love, contempt and disillusionment that confine him to a life lived principally in his mind.

5

Winnicott's "Primitive emotional development"

Psychoanalysis in its first century has had several great thinkers, but, to my mind, only one great English-speaking writer: Donald Winnicott. Because style and content are so interdependent in his writing, his papers are not well served by a thematic reading aimed exclusively at gleaning what the paper is "about." Such efforts often result in trivial aphorisms. Winnicott, for the most part, does not use language to arrive at conclusions; rather, he uses language to create experiences in reading which are inseparable from the ideas he is presenting – or, more accurately, the ideas he is playing with.

I offer here a reading of Winnicott's (1945) "Primitive emotional development," a paper that contains the seeds of virtually all the major contributions to psychoanalysis that Winnicott would make over the course of the succeeding 26 years of his life. I hope to demonstrate the interdependence of the life of the ideas being developed and the life of the writing in this seminal contribution to the analytic literature. What Winnicott's paper has to offer to an analytic reader could not be said in any other way (which is to say that the writing is extraordinarily resistant to paraphrase). It has been my experience that an awareness of the way the language is working significantly enhances what can be learned from reading Winnicott.

In recent years, I have found that the only way I can do justice to studying and teaching Winnicott is to read his papers aloud, line by line, as I would a poem, exploring what the language is doing in addition to what it is saying. It is not an overstatement to say that a great many passages from Winnicott's papers well deserve to be called prose poems. These passages meet Tom Stoppard's (1999) definition

76

of poetry as "the simultaneous compression of language and expansion of meaning" (p. 10).

In my discussion of Winnicott's paper, I will not be limiting myself to an explication of the text, although many of the ideas developed there will be discussed. My principal interest is in looking at this paper as a piece of non-fiction literature in which the meeting of reader and writing generates an imaginative experience in the medium of language. To speak of Winnicott's writing as literature is not to minimize its value as a way of conveying ideas that have proved to be of enormous importance to the development of psychoanalytic theory and practice. On the contrary, my effort is to demonstrate how the life of the writing is critical to, and inseparable from, the life of the ideas.

Before looking closely at "Primitive emotional development," I will offer a few observations about Winnicott's writing that are relevant to the whole of his opus. The first quality of Winnicott's writing that strikes the reader is its form. Unlike the papers of any other psychoanalyst I can think of, Winnicott's papers are brief (usually six to ten pages in length), often containing a moment in the middle of the paper when he takes the reader aside and tells him, in a single sentence, "the essential feature of my communication is this . . ." (Winnicott, 1971b, p. 50). But the most distinctive signature of Winnicott's writing is the voice. It is casual and conversational, but always profoundly respectful of both the reader and the subject matter under discussion. The speaking voice gives itself permission to wander, and yet has the compactness of poetry; there is an extraordinary intelligence to the voice that is at the same time genuinely humble and well aware of its limitations; it has a disarming intimacy that at times takes cover in wit and charm; the voice is playful and imaginative, but never folksy or sentimental.

Any effort to convey a sense of the voice in Winnicott's writing must locate at its core the quality of playfulness, and there is an enormous range of forms of playfulness to be found. To name only a few, there are the unselfconscious feats of imaginative, compassionate understanding in his accounts of "squiggle games" (1971c) with his child patients. There is serious playfulness (or playful seriousness) in the voice when Winnicott is involved in an effort to generate a form of thinking/theorizing that is adequate to the paradoxical nature of human experience as he understands it. Winnicott takes delight in subtle word play, for instance, in the repetition of a familiar phrase in slightly different forms, to refer to the patient's need to begin and to end analysis: "I do analysis because that is what the patient needs to have done and to have done with" (1962, p. 166).

While his writing is personal, there is also a certain English formality to the voice in Winnicott's writing that befits the paradoxical combination of formality and intimacy that is a hallmark of psychoanalysis (Ogden, 1989). In terms of all of these matters of form and voice, Winnicott's work holds strong resemblances to the compact, intelligent, playful, at times charming, at times ironic, always irreducible writing of Borges' *Ficciones* (1944) and Frost's prose and poetry.

Winnicott's inimitable voice can be heard almost immediately in "Primitive emotional development" as he explains his "methodology":

> I shall not first give an historical survey and show the development of my ideas from the theories of others, because my mind does not work that way. What happens is that I gather this and that, here and there, settle down to clinical experience, form my own theories and then, last of all, interest myself in looking to see where I stole what. Perhaps this is as good a method as any.
>
> (p. 145)

There is playful wit to the words, "Perhaps this is as good a method as any." This seemingly tacked-on afterthought expresses what is perhaps the central theme of the paper as a whole: creating "a method," a way of being alive, that suits the individual and becomes his unique "watermarking" (Heaney, 1980, p. 47), is perhaps the single most important outcome of primitive emotional development. In the process of coming into being as an individual, the infant (and mother) "gather this and that, here and there." Early experience of self is fragmented and at the same time is (with the help of the mother) "gather[ed]" in a way that allows the infant's experience of self, now and again, to come together in one place. Moreover, for the infant, the bits of others (introjects) – or, for the writer, the ideas of other writers – must not be allowed to take over the process of creating meaning. "My mind does not work that way," nor does that of the healthy infant in the care of a healthy mother. The individual's own lived experience must be the basis for creating coherence *for* oneself and integrity *of* oneself. Only after a sense of self has begun to come into being (for the infant and for the writer) can one acknowledge the contributions of others to the creating of oneself (and one's ideas): ". . . last of all [I] interest myself in where I stole what."

Winnicott then briefly discusses several aspects of the analytic relationship, with particular emphasis on the transference–countertransference. He believes that the body of experience he has had has been a major source of his conception of primitive emotional development. I will examine only one brief passage (two sentences to be precise) of Winnicott's discussion of the transference–countertransference. I have selected these sentences because I find them to be of enormous importance to the understanding of both Winnicott's conception of the workings of the analytic relationship, and the powerful interdependence of language and ideas in his work:

> The depressed patient requires of his analyst the understanding that the analyst's work is to some extent his effort to cope with his own (the analyst's) depression, or shall I say guilt and grief resultant from the destructive elements in his own (the analyst's) love. To progress further along these lines, the patient who is asking for help in regard to his primitive, pre-depressive relationship to objects needs his analyst to be able to see the analyst's undisplaced and co-incident love and hate of him.
>
> (pp. 146–147)

In the opening clause of the first of these two sentences, Winnicott not only offers a theory of depression radically different from those of Freud and Klein, but also proposes a new conception of the role of countertransference in the psychoanalytic process. Winnicott is suggesting here that depression is not, most fundamentally, a pathological internalization of a narcissistically loved (and lost) object (in an effort to evade experiencing the reality of the loss of the object) (Freud, 1917a, 1917b; see Chapter 2). Neither does the understanding of depression that Winnicott is suggesting view depression as centered around the unconscious fantasy that one's anger has injured, driven away or killed the loved object (Klein, 1952).

In the space of a single sentence, Winnicott suggests (by means of his *use of the idea* rather than through his explication of it) that depression is a manifestation of the patient's taking on as his own – in fantasy, taking into himself – his mother's depression (or that of other loved objects) with the unconscious aim of relieving her of her depression. What is astounding is that this conception of the patient's depression is presented not through a direct statement, but by means of a sentence that is virtually incomprehensible unless the reader does the work of creating/discovering for himself the conception of the intergenerational origins and dynamic structure of depression. Only after the reader has done this work does it begin to make sense why "The depressed patient requires of his analyst the understanding that the analyst's work is to some extent his effort to cope with his own (the analyst's) depression" (pp. 146–147).[1] In other words, if the analyst is unable to cope with his own feelings of depression (both normative and pathological) arising from his own past and current life experiences, he will not be able to recognize (to feel in the moment) the ways in which the patient is unconsciously attempting to, and to some degree succeeding in, taking on the depression of the analyst-as-transference-mother.

The aspects of the analyst's depression that arise from sources independent of his unconscious identification with the patient's depressed internal object mother are far less available to the patient's ministerings because the patient cannot find in the analyst the depression of his (the patient's) mother which for nearly the whole of his life he has intimately known and attended to. The patient is single-mindedly concerned with the depression that is unique to his internal object mother. (Each person's depression is his or her own unique creation rooted in the particular circumstances of his or her own life experience and personality organization.) Winnicott is suggesting that the analyst must cope with his own depression in order that he might experience the patient's (internal object) mother's depression (that is being projected into him). Only if he is able to contain/live with the experience of the (internal object) mother's depression (as distinct from his own depression) will he be able to experience the patient's pathological effort to relieve the mother's psychological pain (now felt to be located in the analyst) by introjecting it into himself (the patient) as a noxious foreign body.

---

1 The term "depression," as it is used in this sentence, seems to refer to a wide spectrum of psychological states ranging from clinical depression to the universal depression associated with the achievement of the depressive position (Klein, 1952). The latter is a normative stage of development and "mode of generating experience" (Ogden, 1989, p. 9) involving whole object relatedness, ambivalence and a deep sense of loss in recognizing one's separateness from one's mother.

The second clause of the sentence being discussed, while introduced by Winnicott as if it were simply another way of saying what
he has already said in the first clause ("or shall I say"), is in fact something altogether new: the analyst of a depressed patient must cope
with his own "guilt and grief resultant from the destructive elements
in his own (the analyst's) love" (p. 146). Thus, the analyst of the
depressed patient must also be able to live with the inevitable destructiveness of love in the sense that love involves a demand on the loved
object which may (in fantasy, and, at times, in reality) be too much
of a strain for the person one loves. In other words, the analyst, in the
course of his personal analysis and by means of his ongoing self-
analysis, must come to terms with his own fears of the draining effects
of his love sufficiently to be able to love his patient without fear that
such feelings will harm the patient and thereby cause himself (the
analyst) "guilt and grief." I am aware of the awkwardness of my own
language in discussing this passage. These ideas are difficult to convey
in part because of the extreme compactness of Winnicott's language
and, in part, because Winnicott has not yet fully worked out the
ideas he is presenting. Moreover, the ideas he is developing here
involve irresolvable emotional contradictions and paradoxes: the
analyst must be sufficiently free of depression to experience the
depression which the depressed patient projects into him. The analyst
must also be able to love without fear of the toll that his love takes
– for if the analyst is frightened of the destructive effects of his own
love, there is little chance of his analyzing the patient's fears of the
taxing/destructive effects of his love on the analyst.

Winnicott does not stop here. In the sentence that follows, he revo-
lutionizes (and I use the word advisedly) the psychoanalytic conception of "the analytic frame" by viewing it as a medium for the
expression of the analyst's hatred of the patient: "the end of the hour,
the end of the analysis, the rules and regulations, these all come in as
expressions of [the analyst's] hate" (p. 147). These words derive a good
deal of their power from the fact that the truth of the idea
that the analyst expresses his hate in these actions (which are so ordinary as to go frequently unnoticed) is immediately recognizable by the
analytic reader as part of his experience with virtually every patient.
Winnicott is recognizing/interpreting the unspoken expressions of
hate that the analyst/reader unconsciously and preconsciously experiences (often accompanied by feelings of relief) in "throwing the patient
out" (by punctually ending each meeting) and by establishing the limits

of what he will provide the patient (by maintaining the other aspects of the analytic frame). Implicit here is the notion that the analyst's fear of the destructiveness of his hatred of the patient may lead to treatment-destructive breaches of the analytic frame: for example, extending the session for more than a few minutes in order "not to cut the patient off," or setting the fee at a level below what the patient is able to afford "because the patient has been consistently exploited by his parents in childhood," or reflexively telephoning the patient when the patient has missed a session "to be sure he is all right," and so on.

Only by looking closely at these sentences can one discern and appreciate what is going on in the very living relationship between the writing and the reader that constitutes so much of the life of the ideas being developed. As we have seen, the writing demands that the reader become an active partner in the creation of meaning. The writing (like the communications of an analysand) suggests, and only suggests, possibilities of meaning. The reader/analyst must be willing and able not to know in order to make room in himself for a number of possible meanings to be experienced/created, and to allow one meaning or another or several meanings concurrently to achieve ascendance (for a time).

Moreover, it is important to note that the writing "works" (to borrow a word from Winnicott's statement of his "method") in large measure by means of its power to understand (to correctly interpret the unconscious of) the reader. Perhaps all good writing (whether it be in poems, plays, novels or essays) to a significant degree "works" in this way.

Winnicott's writing in the paper under discussion (and in almost all of the papers included in his three major volumes of collected papers [1958, 1965, 1971d]) is surprisingly short on clinical material. This, I believe, is a consequence of the fact that the "clinical experience" is to such a large degree located in the reader's experience of "being read" (that is, of being interpreted, understood) by the writing. When Winnicott does offer clinical material, he often refers not to a specific intervention with a particular patient, but to a "very common experience" (1945, p. 150) in analysis. In this way, he implicitly asks the reader to draw on his own lived experience with patients: not for the purpose of "taking in" Winnicott's ideas, but to invite from the reader an "original response" (Frost, 1942a, p. 307).

Still other forms of generative interplay of style and content, of writing and reader, take on central importance in a passage a bit later in the paper which addresses experiences of unintegration and integration in early development:

> An example of unintegration phenomena is provided by the very common experience of the patient who proceeds to give every detail of the week-end and feels contented at the end if everything has been said, though the analyst feels that no analytic work has been done. Sometimes we must interpret this as the patient's need to be known in all his bits and pieces by one person, the analyst. To be known means to feel integrated at least in the person of the analyst. This is the ordinary stuff of infant life, and an infant who has had no one person to gather his bits together starts with a handicap in his own self-integrating task, and perhaps he cannot succeed, or at any rate cannot maintain integration with confidence . . .
>
> There are long stretches of time in a normal infant's life in which a baby does not mind whether he is in many bits or one whole being, or whether he lives in his mother's face or in his own body, provided that from time to time he comes together and feels something.
>
> (p. 150)

Implicit in this passage is the recognition of the analyst's anger at patients who "give every detail of the week-end," leaving the analyst with the feeling "that no analytic work has been done." Winnicott leaves it entirely to the reader to imagine the analyst's impulse to dump his anger and feelings of failure back into the patient in the form of a resistance interpretation ("You seem to be filling the hour with details that serve to defeat any possibility of analytic work getting done" [my example]).

Winnicott then provides the reader with a major revision of analytic technique. He accomplishes this so subtly that the reader is apt not to notice it if he is not attending carefully to what is going on in the writing. Nothing short of a new way of being with and talking to patients is being offered, without preaching or fanfare: "Sometimes we must interpret[2] this [the patient's giving every detail of his week-end]

---

2 It seems to me that Winnicott is referring here to silent interpretations that the analyst formulates in words for himself in the moment and may at a later time present to the patient.

as the patient's need to be known in all his bits and pieces by one person, the analyst." The phrase "Sometimes we must" addresses the reader as a colleague who is familiar with the clinical situation being described, and who very likely has felt it necessary to intervene in the way Winnicott is describing. Perhaps the reader/analyst has not fully named for himself what he has been experiencing and doing with his patient. The language does not debunk the angry resistance interpretation that the reader/analyst has either made or has been inclined to make in response to his feelings of frustration and failure. Winnicott, by means of the language he uses to address the reader, provides *an experience in reading* that helps the reader undefensively to gather together his own unarticulated experiences from his own analysis and from his analytic work with his patients.

Moreover, the simple phrase "very common experience" conveys an important theoretical concept (again without calling attention to itself): primitive states of unintegration are not restricted to the analysis of severely disturbed patients; such states regularly occur in the analysis of all of our patients, including the healthiest ones. This writing "technique" does not have the feel of a manipulation of the reader; rather, it feels like a good interpretation – a statement that puts into words what the reader/analyst has known from his experience all along, but has not known that he has known it, and has not known it in the verbally symbolized, integrated way that he is currently coming to know it.

The second paragraph of the passage being discussed is remarkable:

> There are long stretches of time in a normal infant's life in which a baby does not mind whether he is many bits or one whole being, or whether he lives in his mother's face or in his own body, provided that from time to time he comes together and feels something.
>
> (p. 150)

This sentence is distinctive, not only for the originality of the ideas it develops, but also for the way in which its syntax participates in a sensory way in the creation of those ideas. The sentence is constructed of many (I count ten) groups of words that are read with a very brief pause between them (for instance, a pause after the words "time," "life," "mind," and so on). The sentence not only states, but brings to life in its own audible structure, the experience of living in bits ("for a long time") in a meandering sort of way before coming

84

together (for a moment) in its final two bits: "he comes together" and "feels something." The voice, syntax, rhythm, and carefully chosen words and expressions which constitute this sentence – working together as they do with the ideas being developed – create an experience in reading that is as distinctively Winnicott as the opening paragraph of the *The Sound and the Fury* is distinctively Faulkner, or as the opening sentence of *The Portrait of a Lady* is uniquely Henry James.

The reader of the sentence being discussed is not moved to question how Winnicott can possibly know what an infant feels or to point out that regressions in the analyses of children and adults (whether psychotic, depressed or quite healthy) bear a very uncertain correlation with infantile experience. Rather, the reader is inclined to suspend disbelief for a time and to enter into the experience of reading (with Winnicott) and to allow himself to be carried by the music of the language and ideas. The reader lives an experience (in the act of reading) that is something like that of the imagined infant who does not mind whether he is in many bits (experiencing a floating feeling that accompanies non-linear thinking) or one whole being (experiencing a "momentary stay against confusion" [Frost, 1939, p. 777]). Winnicott's writing, like a guide "who only has at heart your getting lost" (Frost, 1947, p. 341), ensures that we will never get it right in any final way, and we do not mind.

Subliminally, the pun on "mind" allows the clause "a baby does not mind whether he is many bits or one whole being" to concentrate into itself different overlapping meanings. The baby "does not mind" because the mother is there "minding" him (taking care of him). And he "does not mind" in that he feels no pressure to be "minded," that is, to create premature, defensive mindedness which is disconnected from bodily experience. The writing itself, in punning, deftly and unselfconsciously creates just such an experience of the pleasure of not minding, of not having to know, of not having to pin down meaning, instead, simply enjoying the liveliness of a fine experience in the medium of language and ideas.

The language that Winnicott uses in describing the infant's coming together in one place is surprising in that the "place" where coming together occurs is not a place at all, but an action (the act of feeling something). Moreover, the infant, in "coming together," does not simply feel, he "feels something" (p. 150). The word "something" has a delightful ambiguity to it: "something" is a concrete thing, the object that is felt; and, at the same time, "something" is the most indefinite of words suggesting only that some feeling is experienced. This delicate ambiguity creates in the experience of reading the flickering of the feeling-world of the infant, a world loosely bound to objects, loosely localized, experienced now in the body as objectless sensation, now in the more defined and localized sensation of feeling an object, now in the mother's face.[3]

The unexpected turns, the quiet revolutions occurring in this early Winnicott paper are too numerous to address. I cannot resist, however, taking a moment simply to marvel at the way in which Winnicott, the pediatrician, the child-analyst, nonchalantly jettisons the accrued technical language of 50 years of psychoanalytic writing in favor of language that is alive with the experiences he is describing:

> there are the quiet and the excited states. I think an infant cannot be said to be aware at the start that while feeling this and that in his cot or enjoying the skin stimulations of bathing, he is the same as himself screaming for immediate satisfaction, possessed by an urge to get at and destroy something unless satisfied by milk. This means that he does not know at first that the mother he is building up through his quiet experiences is the same as the power behind the breasts that he has in his mind to destroy.
>
> (p. 151)

The infant has his quiet and his excited states – everyone who has spent time with a baby knows this, but why had no one thought to put it this way? The baby feels "this and that" (there is ease in the language as there is ease in the baby's state of mind-body) and enjoys the "skin stimulations of bathing" and "cannot be said to be aware [in the quiet states] . . . that . . . he is the same as himself screaming for immediate satisfaction." (And how better to capture at the same time the underlying continuity of identity across discontinuous feeling/meaning states than with unobtrusive alliteration of "s"

---

3 The role played by the word "something" in this sentence is reminiscent of Frost's use of nouns to simultaneously invoke the mysterious and the utterly concrete and mundane, for example, in lines such as "Something there is that doesn't love a wall" (1914, p. 39) or "One had to be versed in country things/Not to believe the phoebes wept" (1923a, p. 223) or "What was that whiteness?/ Truth? A pebble of quartz? For once, then, something" (1923b, p. 208).

sounds – 16 times in one sentence – in words carrying a very wide range of meaning: "states," "start," "skin," "stimulation," "same," "screaming," "satisfaction," "something," and "satisfied?")[4]

Winnicott continues:

> Also I think there is not necessarily an integration between a child asleep and a child awake . . . Once dreams are remembered and even conveyed somehow to a third person, the dissociation is broken down a little; but some people never clearly remember their dreams, and children depend very much on adults for getting to know their dreams. It is normal for small children to have anxiety dreams and terrors. At these times, children need someone to help them to remember what they dreamed. It is a valuable experience whenever a dream is both dreamed *and* remembered, precisely because of the breakdown of dissociation that this represents.
>
> (p. 151).

In this part of the paper, Winnicott speaks of how important it is for a child to have the experience of conveying his dream "somehow to a third person." Every time I read this sentence, I find it jarring and confusing. I attempt to account for a third person in the apparently two-person experience of a dream (not yet the child's creation or possession) being "conveyed somehow" to a third person. Is the third person the experience of the father's symbolic presence even in his absence? Perhaps, but such an idea seems too much an experience of the mind disconnected from the bodily feel, the sense of aliveness that one experiences when engaging with a child in spoken or unspoken conversation. A dream unobtrusively can be entered into a conversation or into playing, sometimes wordlessly, because the child *is* the dream before the dream is his. Thus, the three people are,

---

4 Of course, I am not suggesting that Winnicott planned, or even was aware of, the way he was using alliteration, syntax, rhythm, punning and so on to create specific effects in his use of language any more than a talented poet plans ahead of time which metaphors, images, rhymes, rhythms, meters, syntactical structures, diction, allusions, line lengths and so on that he will use. The act of writing seems to have a life of its own. It is one of the "rights and privileges," as well as one of the pleasures, of critical reading to attempt to discern what is going on in a piece of writing – regardless of whether the writer intended it or was even cognizant of it.

from this perspective, the dreaming child, the waking child and the adult. This interpretation is suggested by the language, but the reader, once again, must do the work of imaginatively entering into the experience of reading. The language quietly creates (as opposed to discusses) the confusion that the reader/child experiences about how many people are present in the act of conveying a dream to an adult. The reader experiences what it feels like for a child to be two people and not to notice that experience until an adult gives him help in "getting to know [what are becoming *his*] dreams" (p. 151). "Getting to know" his dreams – the expression is uniquely Winnicott; no one else could have written these words. The phrase is implicitly a metaphor in which an adult "makes the introductions" in the first meeting of a waking child and his dreams. In this imaginary social event, not only is the child learning that he has a dream-life, his unconscious is learning that "it" (which in health is forever in the process of becoming "I") has a "waking-life."

The metaphorical language of this passage is carrying a heavy theoretical load without the slightest evidence of strain. First of all, there is the matter that, as Freud put it, the unconscious "is alive" (1915c, p. 190), and consequently "getting to know" one's dreams is no less than the beginnings of healthy communication at the "frontier" (Freud, 1915c, p. 193) of the unconscious and preconscious mind. As the waking child and the dreaming child become acquainted with one another (i.e. as the child comes to experience himself as the same person who has both a waking-life and a dream-life), the experience of dreaming feels less strange (other to oneself) and hence less frightening.[5]

It might be said that when a dream is both dreamed and remembered, the conversation between the conscious-preconscious and the unconscious aspects of mind "across the repression barrier" is enhanced. But once it is put in these terms, the reasons for enjoying Winnicott's writing become all the more apparent. In contrast to the noun-laden language of *preconscious, conscious, unconscious, repression* and so on, Winnicott's language seems to be all verb: "feeling something," "getting to know their dreams," "screaming," "possessed."

---

5 Even as adults, we never completely experience dream-life and waking-life as two different forms of the experience of ourselves as one person. This is reflected in the language we use in talking about dreams. For example, we say "I had a dream last night" [it happened to me] and not "I made a dream last night."

Having discussed the infant's early experience of coming together (in health) from his experience of living in bits and pieces (unintegration) and from a variety of forms of dissociation (e.g. the dissociation of dreaming and waking states), Winnicott turns to the infant's experience of his earliest relations with external reality:

> In terms of baby and mother's breast (I am not claiming that the breast is essential as a vehicle of mother-love) the baby has instinctual urges and predatory ideas. The mother has a breast and the power to produce milk, and the idea that she would like to be attacked by a hungry baby. These two phenomena do not come into relation with each other till the mother and child *live an experience together*. The mother being mature and physically able has to be the one with tolerance and understanding, so that it is she who produces a situation that may with luck result in the first tie the infant makes with an external object, an object that is external to the self from the infant's point of view.
>
> (p. 152)

In this passage the language is doing far more than is apparent. "The baby [at this juncture] has instinctual urges and predatory ideas. The mother [with an internal life quite separate from that of the infant] has a breast and the power to produce milk, and the idea that she would like to be attacked by a hungry baby." The deadly seriousness (and violence) of these words – instinctual urges, predatory, power, attack – plays off against the whimsy and humor of the intentionally over-drawn images. The notion of a baby with "predatory ideas" conjures up images of a scheming mastermind criminal in diapers. And, in a similar way, the notion of a mother who would like to be "attacked by a hungry baby" stirs up images of a mother (her large breasts engorged with milk) walking through dimly-lit alleys at night hoping to be violently assaulted by a hoodlum baby with a terrible craving for milk. The language, at once serious and playful (at times even ridiculous), creates a sense of the complementarity of the internal states of mother and infant: a complementarity that is going on only in parallel, and not yet in relation to one another.

In the sentence that immediately follows, we find one of Winnicott's most important theoretical contributions to psychoanalysis, an idea that has significantly shaped the subsequent 65 years of the history of analytic thought. As the idea is rendered here, it is, to my mind, even more richly suggestive than it is in its later, more familiar forms: "These two phenomena [the infant with his predatory urges and ideas and the mother with her instinctual urges and her wish to be attacked by a hungry baby] do not come into relation with each other till the mother and child *live an experience together*" (p. 152).

"*Live an experience together*" – what makes the phrase remarkable is the unexpected word "live." The mother and child do not "take part in," "share," "participate in" or "enter into" an experience together: they live an experience together. In this single phrase, Winnicott is suggesting (though I think he is not fully aware of this as he writes this paper) that he is in the process of transforming psychoanalysis, both as a theory and as a therapeutic relationship, in a way that involves altering the notion of what is most fundamental to human psychology. No longer will it be desiring and regulating desire [Freud], loving, hating, and making reparations [Klein], or object-seeking and object-relating [Fairbairn] that are of greatest importance in the development of the psyche–soma from its beginnings and continuing throughout life. Instead, what Winnicott is beginning to lay out here for the first time is the idea that the central organizing thread of psychological development from its inception is the experience of being alive and the consequences of disruptions to that continuity of being.

The specific way in which Winnicott uses language in this passage is critical to the nature of the meanings being generated. In the phrase "live an experience together," "live" is a transitive verb, which takes "experience" as its object. Living an experience is an act of doing something to someone or something (as much as the act of hitting a ball is an act of doing something to the ball); it is an act of infusing experience with life. Human experience does not have life until we live it (as opposed to simply having it in an operational way). Mother and child do not come into relation to one another until they each *do something* to experience, that is, they live it *together* (not simply at the same time, but while experiencing and responding to one another's separate act of being alive in living the experience).

The paragraph concludes: "The mother being mature and physically able has to be the one with tolerance and understanding, so that it is she who produces a situation that may with luck result in the first tie the infant makes with an external object, an object that is external to the self from the infant's point of view" (p. 152). The unstated paradox that emerges here involves the idea that living an experience *together* serves to *separate* the mother and infant (to bring them, from the infant's perspective, "into relation with each other" as separate entities). This paradox lies at the heart of the experience of illusion: "I think of the process as if two lines came from opposite directions, liable to come near each other. If they overlap, there is a moment of *illusion* – a bit of experience which the infant can take as *either* his hallucination *or* a thing belonging to external reality" (p. 152).

Of course, what is being introduced is the concept that Winnicott (1951) later termed "transitional phenomena." The "moment of illusion" is a moment of psychological "overlap" of the mother and infant – a moment in which the mother lives an experience with the infant in which she actively/unconsciously/naturally provides herself as an object that can be experienced by the infant at once as his creation (an unnoticed experience because there is nothing that is *not* what is expected) *and* as his discovery (an event with a quality of otherness in a world external to his sense of self).

> In other language, the infant comes to the breast when excited, and ready to hallucinate something fit to be attacked. At that moment, the actual nipple appears and he is able to feel it was that nipple that he hallucinated. So his ideas are enriched by actual details of sight, feel, smell, and next time this material is used in the hallucination. In this way he starts to build a capacity to conjure up what is actually available. The mother has to go on giving the infant this type of experience.
>
> (pp. 152–153)

What Winnicott is attempting to describe (and succeeds in capturing in his use of language) is not simply an experience, but a *way* of experiencing that is lighter, more full of darting energy, than other ways of experiencing. The initial metaphor that Winnicott uses to introduce this way of experiencing involves the image of mother and infant as two lines (or is it lives?) coming from opposite directions (from the world of magic and from the world of grounded consensual reality) which are "liable to come near each other" (p. 152). The word "liable" is unexpected with its connotations of chance events (perhaps of an unwelcome nature?). Is there a hint of irony about accidents being a port of entry into the "real world"?

For Winnicott, the maternal provision is even more complex than that of creating a psychological–interpersonal field in which the infant gains entry at the same moment into external reality, internal reality and the experience of illusion. The mother's task at this stage of things also involves protecting "her infant from complications that cannot yet be understood by the infant" (p. 153). "Complications" is a word newly made in this sentence. In Winnicott's hands, the word "complications" takes on a rather specific set of meanings having to do with a convergence of internal and external stimuli that are related to each other in ways that are beyond the capacity of the infant to understand. A few years later, speaking of the mother's efforts "not to introduce complications beyond what the infant can understand and allow for," Winnicott adds: "in particular she tries to insulate her baby from coincidences" (1949, p. 245). "Coincidences" is a word even more richly enigmatic than "complications." It is a word with a long and troubling history in Western myth and literature. (Sophocles' version of the Oedipus myth represents only one instance of the ruin that "coincidence" can leave in its wake.)

Winnicott does not explain what he means by "coincidences" or "complications," much less how one goes about insulating babies from them. His indefinite, enigmatic language does not fill a space with knowledge, it opens up a space for thinking, imagining and freshly experiencing. One possible reading of the words "complications" and "coincidences" (as Winnicott is using/creating them) that I sometimes find useful goes as follows: The coincidences or complications from which a baby needs to be insulated involve chance simultaneities of events taking place in the infant's internal and external realities at a time when the two are only beginning to be differentiated from one another. For instance, a hungry infant may become both fearful and rageful as he waits for his mother longer than he can tolerate. The mother may be feeling preoccupied and distraught for reasons that have nothing to do with the infant – perhaps as a consequence of a recent argument with her husband, or physical pain that she fears is a symptom of a serious illness. The simultaneity of the internal event (the infant's hunger, fear, rage) and the external event (the mother's emotional absence) is a coincidence that the infant cannot understand. He makes sense of it by imagining that it is his own anger and predatory urges that have killed the mother. The mother who had earlier wished to be attacked by a hungry baby is gone and in her place is a lifeless mother passively allowing herself to be attacked by the hungry baby as carrion is available for consumption by vultures.

"Coincidence" leads the infant defensively to bring a degree of order and control to his experience by drawing what was becoming the external world back into his internal world by means of omnipotent fantasy: "I killed her." In contrast, when a mother and child are able to "live an experience together," the vitality of the child's internal world is recognized and met by the external world (the mother's act of living the experience together with him). Winnicott does not state these ideas as such, but they are there to be found/created by the reader.

A note of caution is needed here with regard to the license a reader may take in creating a text and that caveat is provided by Winnicott. It is implicit in all of Winnicott's writing that creativity must not be valorized above all else. Creativity is not only worthless, it is lethal (literally so in the case of an infant) when disconnected from objectivity – that is, from "acceptance of external reality" (p. 53). An infant forever hallucinating what he needs will starve to death; a reader who loses touch with the writing will not be able to learn from it.

Winnicott's conception of the infant's earliest experience of accepting external reality is as beautifully rendered as it is subtle in content:

> One thing that follows the acceptance of external reality is the advantage to be gained from it. We often hear of the very real frustrations imposed by external reality, but less often hear of the relief and satisfaction it affords. Real milk is satisfying as compared with imaginary milk, but this is not the point. The point is that in fantasy things work by magic: there are no brakes on fantasy, and love and hate cause alarming effects. External reality has brakes on it, and can be studied and known, and, in fact, fantasy is only tolerable at full blast when objective reality is appreciated well. The subjective has tremendous value but is so alarming and magical that it cannot be enjoyed except as a parallel to the objective.
>
> (p. 153)

This is a muscular passage. After acknowledging what is already self-evident ("Real milk is satisfying as compared to imaginary milk"), the passage seems to break open mid-sentence: "but this is not the point. The point is that in fantasy things work by magic: there are no brakes on fantasy, and love and hate cause alarming effects." External reality is not simply an abstraction in these sentences; it is alive in the language. It is a felt presence in the sound of the words – for instance, in the dense, cold metallic sound of the word "brakes" (which evokes in me the image of a locomotive with wheels locked screeching to a halt over smooth iron tracks). The metaphor of a vehicle without the means to be stopped (a metaphor implicit in the words "without brakes") is elaborated as the sentence proceeds: "love and hate cause alarming effects." Love and hate are without a subject, thus making the metaphorical vehicle not only without brakes but also without a driver (or engineer).

The modulating effects of external reality can be felt in the restraint and frequent pauses in the first half of the sentence that immediately follows: "External reality has brakes on it, [–] and can be studied and known [–], and [–], in fact [–] . . ." (p. 153). Having been slowed, the sentence (and the experience of internal and external reality) unfolds in a more flowing (which is not to say bland or lifeless) way: "fantasy is only tolerable at full blast when objective reality is appreciated well."

Winnicott returns to the subject of illusion again and again in "Primitive emotional development," each time viewing it from a somewhat different perspective. He is without peer in his ability to capture in words what illusion might feel like to a baby. For instance, on returning to the subject late in the paper, he says that for illusion to be generated, "a simple *contact* with external or shared reality has to be made by the infant's hallucinating and the world's presenting, with moments of illusion for the infant in which the two are taken by him to be identical, which they never in fact are" (p. 154). For this to happen, someone "has to be taking the trouble [a wonderfully simple way to acknowledge the fact that being mother to an infant is a lot of work and a lot of trouble] all the time [even when she longs for even an hour of sleep] to bring the world to the baby in understandable form [without too many complications and coincidences], and in a limited way, suitable to the baby's needs" (p. 154). The rhythm of the series of clauses making up this sentence heaps requirement upon requirement that the mother must meet in creating illusion for the baby. These efforts of the mother constitute the intense backstage labor necessary if the infant is to enjoy his orchestra seat in the performance of illusion. The performance reveals not a hint of the dirty grunt work that creates and safeguards the life of the illusion.

The humor of the contrast between illusion as seen from backstage and from an orchestra seat is I think not at all lost upon Winnicott. The juxtaposition of the passage just quoted (something of a job description for the mother of a baby) and the paragraph that follows (which captures all of the sense of wonder and amazement a child feels on seeing a magic show) can hardly be a coincidence: "The subject of illusion . . . will be found to provide the clue to a child's interest in bubbles and clouds and rainbows and all mysterious phenomena, and also to his interest in fluff. . . . Somewhere here, too, is the interest in breath, which never decides whether it comes primarily from within or without" (p. 154). I am not aware of a comparable expression in all of the analytic literature of the almost translucent, mystifying quality of imaginative experience which becomes possible when the full blast to fantasy is made safe by a child's sturdy grasp on external reality.

Concluding comments

In this, the first of his major papers, Winnicott quietly, unassumingly defies the conventional wisdom which holds writing to be primarily a means to an end: a means by which analytic data and ideas are conveyed to readers as telephones and telephone lines transport the voice in the form of electrical impulses and sound waves. The notion that our experiences as analysts and the ideas with which we make sense of them are inseparable from the language we use to create/ convey them is an idea that some analysts strenuously resist. For them, it is disappointing to acknowledge that discourse among analysts, whether written or spoken, will forever remain limited by our imprecise, impressionistic (and consequently confusing and misleading) accounts of what we observe and how we think about what we do as psychoanalysts. For others, the inseparability of our observations and ideas, on the one hand, and the language we use to express them, on the other, is an exciting idea − it embraces the indissoluble interpenetration of life and art, neither preceding the other, neither holding dominion over the other. To be alive (in more than an operational sense) is to be forever in the process of making things of one's own, whether they be thoughts, feelings, bodily movements, perceptions, conversations, poems or analytic papers. No psychoanalyst's writing bears witness better than Winnicott's to the mutually dependent, mutually enlivening relationship of life and art.

6

Reading Bion

Bion's writing is difficult: often turgid, frequently confounding (maddeningly so), and regularly mystifying. And yet, I find that my attempts to paraphrase his writing almost always leave me feeling that I have lost what is most important to Bion's thinking. I offer here some thoughts on how, over the years, I have come to read Bion, which I hope will be of help to others in their efforts at finding their own ways to read his work. Perhaps most important to the way I read his work is the state of mind I try to bring to it – a state of mind in which I fully accept what I believe to be Bion's view of his own writing: he strives not to be understood, but to serve as a catalyst for the reader's own thinking.

A second orienting idea that I bring to my reading of Bion is a conception of Bion's opus as being comprised of two periods that I think of as "early" and "late" Bion. I view the writing in the two periods as based on overlapping, yet distinctly different sets of assumptions regarding psychoanalysis. The writing from the two periods requires different ways of reading, which generate different experiences in reading. I believe that much confusion is generated if the reader treats Bion's early and late work as constituting a gradual unfolding of ideas that are continuous in their view of psychological development. To my mind, the late work, while incorporating and assuming a thorough familiarity with the early work, represents a radical departure from it. "Early Bion," as I conceive of this body of work, consists of all of his writing up to and including *Learning from Experience* (1962a); "late Bion" begins with *Elements of Psycho-Analysis* (1963) and continues through the remainder of his work (in which *Attention and Interpretation* [1970] stands as the major contribution).

97

In this essay on reading Bion, I take as starting points the experience of reading two passages, one from *Learning from Experience* (1962a) and the other from *Attention and Interpretation* (1970). In these passages, Bion suggests to the reader the way he would like his "early" and "late" writing to be read. In this endeavor, I am not attempting to arrive at what Bion "really meant"; rather, I am interested in seeing what use – clinically and theoretically – I am able to make of my own experiences of reading early and late Bion. On the basis of many comments made by Bion in the last decade of his life, there can be little doubt that this is the way Bion would hope to have all of his work read: "The way that *I* do analysis is of no importance to anybody excepting myself, but it may give you some idea of how *you* do analysis, and that *is* important" (1978, p. 206).

In the final section of this chapter, I present a detailed account of an analytic session and then discuss the analytic experience from a point of view that is informed by Bion's work, particularly his late work.

Bion on reading early Bion

In the introduction to *Learning from Experience*, Bion carefully and patiently explains to the reader how he would like this book to be read:

> The book is designed to be read straight through once without checking at parts that might be obscure at first. Some obscurities are due to the impossibility of writing without pre-supposing familiarity with some aspect of a problem that is only worked on later. If the reader will read straight through, those points will become clearer as he proceeds. Unfortunately obscurities also exist because of my inability to make them clearer. The reader may find the effort to clarify these for himself is rewarding and not simply work that has been forced on him because I have not done it myself.
>
> (1962a, p. ii)

In this passage, Bion, in a highly compact way, provides several thoughts on reading his text. First, the reader must be able to tolerate not knowing, getting lost, being confused and pressing ahead anyway. The words "obscure," "obscurities" (mentioned twice), "clearer" and "clarify" (each also used twice) pile up in these five sentences. What it is to learn from experience (or the inability to do so) will be something for the reader to experience first-hand in the act of reading this book – an experience in reading that does not simply "progress" from obscurity to clarification, but resides in a continuous process of clarification negating obscurity and obscurity negating clarification. Bion, not without an edge of irony and wit, suggests that the reader "may find [it] . . . rewarding" to attempt to "clarify [obscurities]" for himself "not simply because I have not done it myself." In other words, if the reader is to engage in something more than "merely reading" (1962a, p. ii) this book, he must become the author of his own book (his own set of thoughts) more or less based on Bion's. Only then will the reader have generated the possibility of learning from his experience of reading.

Bion (1992), in a note to himself, a "cogitation" which in all probability was written during the period in which he was writing *Learning from Experience*, elaborates on the idea that the act of reading is an experience in its own right to be lived and learned from: "A book would have failed for the reader if it does not become an object of study, and the reading of it an emotional experience in itself" (1992, p. 261). In another "cogitation," Bion presents his "early" conception of how analytic writing works, and by implication, how he would like to be read. (The passage I will cite immediately follows a brief page-and-a-half account of an analytic session that includes detailed observations of both Bion's emotional experience and that of his psychotic patient.)

> I do not feel able to communicate to the reader an account that would be likely to satisfy me as correct. I am more confident that I could make the reader understand what I had to put up with if I could extract from him a promise that he would faithfully read every word I wrote; I would then set about writing several hundred thousand words virtually indistinguishable from what I have already written in my account of the two sessions. In short, I cannot have as much confidence in my ability to tell the reader what happened as I have in my ability to do something to the reader that I have had done to me. I have had an emotional experience; I feel confident in my ability to recreate that emotional experience, but not to represent it.
>
> (1992, p. 219)

In this elegant prose – Bion is a difficult writer, not a bad writer – Bion envisions psychoanalytic writing as an effort not to report, but to create an emotional experience that is very close to the emotional experience that the analyst has had in the analysis. In this passage, and the clinical account that precedes it, Bion is doing what he is saying; he is demonstrating as opposed to describing. In the clinical work presented, the psychotic patient, "who [in reality] may commit a murder" (p. 218), whispers at the end of the session, "I will not stand it" (p. 219). Bion comments that "there seems to be no reason such sessions should ever come to an end" (p. 219). (In this last sentence, Bion is speaking from the patient's point of view and in so doing communicates what is unstated in the sentence and in the session, and yet is ominously present in both: in a psychotic field, time is obliterated and endings are arbitrary and unexpected – and consequently may incite actual murder.)

In his comments following the clinical account, Bion succeeds at getting into the language itself something of his experience of being with the patient. He imagines writing several hundred thousand words about "what I had to put up with" and "extract[ing]" – a word that is alive with the sound of violent coercion – "a promise" from the reader. The promise "that [the reader] would faithfully read every word I wrote" is "extract[ed]" before the reader knows of the forthcoming onslaught of words – words that add nothing to what Bion has already said. The experience in reading that Bion is imagining is a tortured one – one that would never come to an end and may incite murderous feelings in the reader. In this way, Bion creates something like the emotional experience he lived with his patient, as opposed to "represent[ing]" it (i.e. describing it). To describe the analytic experience would be to mispresent it because the emotional vantage point of the writing would be from a place outside of the experience, when, in fact, Bion's experience was simultaneously generated from within and outside of the analytic event: "We [analysts] must be able to have these strong feelings *and* be able to go on thinking clearly even when we have them" (Bion, 1978, p. 187).

To summarize, in offering his thoughts on how he would like *Learning from Experience* to be read, Bion portrays a state of mind (generated in the act of reading) that is at once open to living an emotional experience and at the same time actively engaged in clarifying obscurities and obscuring (i.e. releasing itself from the closures of) clarifications. These mental activities in concert constitute a substantial part of what it means to learn from experience, both in reading and in the analytic situation. This is at core a hermeneutic *[interpreta-tion]* approach in which there is a progressive dialectical movement between obscurity and clarification which moves toward, though never achieves, closure.

A mixing of tongues

In examining the emotional experience of reading *Learning from Experience*, it is impossible to ignore the strangeness of the language and terminology that Bion employs. In part, he is attempting to cleanse analytic terminology of the ossified and ossifying "penumbra of associations" (1962a, p. 2) that have accrued over time, and instead, to use "meaningless term[s]" (p. 3) (such as alpha- and beta-elements) unsaturated by previous usage. However, not all of the strangeness of Bion's language is attributable to that effort to generate analytic language disencumbered by accretions of meaning. A large part of the opacity of Bion's writing derives from his mixing the language, notational systems and conceptions belonging to the fields of mathematics and symbolic logic (for example, the concepts of functions and factors) with the language of psychoanalysis.

Bion refers again and again to the set of ideas that he is developing in *Learning from Experience* as "a theory of functions" (p. 2) and devotes much of the first two chapters of the book to explaining what he means by a function. Bion uses the term "function" to refer to a form of mental operation that determines the outcome of every psychic event governed by that mental operation. In mathematics, addition, subtraction, multiplication and division (along with differential and integral calculus) are functions. So when we say $a + b = c$, we are saying that when the function of addition (represented by the $+$ sign) is in operation, we know the relationship among a, b and c. In *Learning from Experience*, Bion is attempting to release psychoanalytic thinking from the confines of the specifics of a given analytic event, thus facilitating the delineation of a small number of essential psychological functions which are very roughly analogous to mathematical functions. This conception of the task of analytic theory accounts for the highly abstract nature of Bion's writing and the paucity of clinical material presented in his work. (Mathematics, according to Bion, could not have developed as a system of logical thought if it required the presence of five oranges to add two and three to make five.)

The way the mind works, from the perspective of "early Bion," centrally involves alpha-function – the function of transforming raw sensory data (termed "beta-elements") into units of meaningful experience (termed "alpha-elements") which can be linked in the process of thinking and stored as memory. As I have previously discussed (Ogden, 2003a), for Bion, dreaming is a form of alpha-function. Dreaming is not a reflection of the differentiation of the conscious and unconscious mind, but the psychological activity/function which generates that differentiation (and consequently is responsible for the maintenance of sanity itself). If one is unable to transform raw sensory data into unconscious elements of experience (alpha-elements), one is unable to dream, unable to differentiate being awake and dreaming; consequently, one is unable to go to sleep and unable to wake up: "hence the peculiar condition seen clinically when the psychotic patient behaves as if he were in precisely this state" (Bion, 1962a, p. 7). (See Ogden, 2003a, for a detailed clinical illustration of analytic work related to the state of not being able to dream.)

I have elected to discuss briefly Bion's theory of functions not only because it represents a critically important aspect of Bion's thinking, but, as important, because it serves as an illustration of the sort of work involved in reading early Bion. The reader must move with Bion as he borrows the concept of function from mathematics and symbolic logic and in so doing moves analytic theory-making to a very high level of abstraction. (This aspect of reading Bion strongly carries over to the experience of reading his theory of transformations and his conception of the grid in his late work.) At the same time, he replaces familiar psychoanalytic models and terminology (e.g. Freud's topographic and structural models and Klein's conception of the paranoid schizoid and depressive positions) with intentionally meaningless terms such as alpha-function, beta-elements and alpha-elements. Moreover, as if this were not sufficiently dislocating for the reader, Bion alters the meanings of everyday words that the reader thought he understood (for instance, the idea of dreaming, going to sleep and waking up).

What is involved in the experience of reading early Bion includes an oscillation between clarification of obscurities and the obscuring of clarifications in a progressive hermeneutic cycle. In addition, the

102

experience of learning from the reading of that work has something of an *Alice in Wonderland* quality. The whole world of psychoanalytic theory feels different as one reads Bion because it is different. Words and ideas once familiar are made foreign, and the foreign made "familiar" ("of the family" of psychoanalytic ideas). How fundamentally different current analytic theory and practice is as a consequence of Bion's early work: for instance, the notion of the patient's attacks on his own meaning-generating function (i.e. his capacity for thinking, feeling, dreaming and so on); the conception of the patient's attacks on the analyst's capacity for reverie; and the delineation of forms of countertransference acting out in which the analyst fearfully and defensively attacks his own and/or the patient's capacity to think.

Bion on reading late Bion

In approaching Bion's late work I will again make use of some of his comments on how he would like his work to be read as a port of entry into his thinking – this time, focusing on *Attention and Interpretation* (1970). A problem posed by Bion's later work is immediately apparent in the "advice" that he offers the reader early in that book. Just as the experience of reading served as a medium in which learning from experience was brought to life in Bion's early work, so too, in *Attention and Interpretation*, the living experience *in reading*[1] is used to convey what cannot be said in words and sentences:

> the reader must disregard what I say until the O of the experience of reading has evolved to a point where the actual events of reading issue in his [the reader's] interpretation of the experiences. Too great a regard for what I have written obstructs the process I represent by the terms 'he becomes the O that is common to himself and myself'.
>
> (1970, p. 28)

---

1 The difference between *thinking about* an experience and *being in* an experience is a recurrent theme in *Attention and Interpretation*, particularly as it relates to the impossibility of becoming an analyst by learning *about* analysis; one must be *in* psychoanalysis – one's own and the analyses one conducts – to be genuinely in the process of becoming a psychoanalyst.

The reader is thrown directly into the fire of not knowing and is advised not to evade this state by holding "too great a regard for what I have written." And at the same time, the question is inescapable: What does Bion mean by "the O" of an experience? He uses such terms as "the thing in itself," "the Truth," "Reality," and "the experience" to convey a sense of what he has in mind by O. But since Bion also insists that O is unknowable, unnamable, beyond human apprehension, these nouns are misleading and contrary to the nature of O. In introducing O to the analytic lexicon, Bion is not proposing another reality "behind" the apprehensible one; he is referring to the reality of what is, a reality that we do not create, a reality that precedes and follows us, and is independent of any human act of knowing, perceiving or apprehending.

The language Bion uses in offering thoughts about reading his late work suggests that the reader is best armed with capacities for the negative. What cannot be known can be addressed only in terms of what it is not: "The reader must disregard what I say" and not hold "too great a regard for what I have written." The "instructions" to the reader in *Learning from Experience* were founded in part on the notion that the reader must let go of what he thought he knew in order to enter a progressive cycle of knowing and not knowing. In contrast, Bion's instructions in *Attention and Interpretation* focus on "disregard[ing]" what Bion is *saying* altogether, for such adherence to statements *about* experience obstructs the reader's access to the actual events [the O of the experience] of reading.

The reader is told that if he is able to remain *in* the experience of reading, his state of mind will "issue in his [the reader's] interpretation of the experiences" (p. 28). The word "experiences" is ambiguous in a critically important way: the word refers both to the analytic experiences he (Bion) has had with his patients, who are now the subject of his text, and to "the experiences" the reader is having in reading the text. Bion's experiences in analysis are conveyed not by writing *about* those experiences, but by using language in such a way that his experiences *in* analysis become the reader's experiences *in* reading. To the extent that the writing works, the irreducible, unverbalizable essence, the O, of each of the two experiences – Bion's experiences in reading his patients and the reader's experience in reading Bion – becomes at one with ("common to") the another. The reader "becomes the O that is common to himself [his experiences in reading] and myself [Bion's experiences *in* the analyses that he has conducted]" (p. 28). I am aware that in the previous sentences, I am using the term O without having defined it. To my mind, this is the only way one can fruitfully approach the concept of O – by allowing its meanings to emerge (its effects to be experienced) as one goes. The effects are ephemeral and survive only as long as the present moment, for no experience can be stored and called up again. We register experience (O) and are altered by it; we hold experience (O) in our being, not in our memory.

Bion's choice of the word "interpretation" in his advice to the reader – "the actual events of reading issue in his interpretation of the experiences" – is unexpected given that the passage strongly privileges "being *in*" as opposed to "speaking *about*." But there is no getting around Bion's use of the nettlesome word "interpretation," which inescapably focuses on the analyst's formulation of what is true to the emotional experience occurring between patient and analyst. What Bion is struggling to convey, I believe, is that psychoanalysis is most fundamentally an enterprise involving "the emergence" (p. 28) into the realm of knowing (K)[2] of the unsymbolizable, unknowable, inexpressible experience itself. Bion's use of the word "emergence" lies at the core of an understanding of the relationship between the experience – the unknowable and unsymbolizable (O) – and the symbolizable, apprehensible dimensions of experience (K).

An emergence is "an unforeseen experience" (*OED*). In terms of the relationship between O and K, experiences in K (i.e. experiences of thinking, feeling, perceiving, apprehending, understanding, remembering and bodily sensing) are "evolutions of O" (p. 27). Such evolutions of O are "unforeseeable" in the same way that consciousness is a wholly unforeseeable emergence from the electrical and chemical workings of the brain. There is absolutely nothing in the study of the physiology of the brain that would lead one to anticipate the experience of human consciousness. Similarly, there is nothing in the structure and physiology of the eye and its myriad connections with the brain that would allow us to anticipate the experience of vision.

---

2 K is a sign used by Bion (1962a) – as I interpret him – to refer not to the noun *knowledge* (a static body of ideas), but to *knowing* (or getting to know), i.e. the effort to be receptive to and give apprehensible form (however inadequate) to what is true to an experience (O).

The idea of "emergence" as a philosophical concept involves a conception of an interplay of forces at one level of complexity (e.g. neuronal clusters) that results in the generation of genuinely novel qualities (e.g. consciousness or vision) that are impossible to antici-pate through the study of the individual units of either of the two levels of complexity (Tresan, 1996; Cambray, 2002). Though there is no evidence that Bion was familiar with this strand of philosophical thought (developed by a group of British philosophers in the first half of the twentieth century [McLaughlin, 1992]), to my mind, the phil-osophical concept of emergence closely corresponds to Bion's (1970) notion of the "emergence" (p. 28) or "evolution" (p. 27) of O in the realm of apprehensible, "sensible" experience (K).

In contrast to the apprehensible evolutions/emergences of O in K, the experience itself (O) simply is. The only verb suited to follow the sign O is some form of the verb to be; an experience in O is an experience of being and becoming. The interpretation as an act of becoming draws on and allows itself to be shaped by what is. One recognizes the truth when one hears it in music, sees it in sculpture, senses it in an analytic interpretation or a dream. One cannot say what it is, but in sculpture, for example, the sculptor creates aesthetic gestures that direct the viewer toward O; in psycho-analysis, the analyst and analysand make "things" (analytic objects such as interpretations) in verbal and non-verbal form that emerge from, and gesture toward, what is true to the present emotional experience.

The O (the truth of what is) is highly specific to the emotional situation generated by a particular analyst and a particular patient at a given moment of analysis. And, at the same time, the truth of what is (the O of that experience) involves a truth that holds for all human-kind from the "past unknown to us . . . [to the] whole present . . . which envelops us all; . . . [to the] future as yet uncreated" (Borges, 1984, p. 63).[3] The O of these universal truths is emergent in and constitutive of our very being and traverses all time, for truth and time are related only by coincidence. In this sense, O is that set of inarticulate, universal human truths that we live, but do not know; it

---

3 For both Bion and Borges the future is already alive in the present as "the as-yet unknown" (Bion, 1970, p. 11); the future casts its shadow backwards on the present (Bion, 1976; Ogden, 2003b).

is what we hear in music and poetry, but cannot name; it is who we are in dreaming, but cannot communicate in the telling of the dream.

O is a state of being-in-the-present-moment, a moment that "Is too present for the senses, / too crowding, too confusing – / too present to imagine" (Frost, 1942b, p. 305). Our capacity for being-in-the-present is "obstructed" by the humanly understandable wish to protect ourselves from its blinding glare. We seek shelter from the O of the present moment in the shadows of memories of what we think we know because it has already been, and in our projections of the past into the future.

It is not surprising, given what I have said, that interpretations that "issue from" the experiences of reading late Bion (or from experiences with a patient in analysis) will inevitably be disappointing and will involve a sense of loss. Bion (1975) has observed that interpretations are regularly followed by a feeling of depression (I would say sadness). What has been lost in the interpretation is the ineffable, inexpressible quality of what is true to the emotional experience. The literary critic Lionel Trilling (1947), in response to the question, "What does *Hamlet* mean?" stated that *Hamlet* does not mean "anything less than *Hamlet*" (p. 49). *Hamlet* is *Hamlet*; O is O; "The world unfortunately is real; I unfortunately am Borges" (Borges, 1962, p. 234).

In sum, Bion's late work requires a type of reading quite different from what is demanded by his early work. Reading the earlier work involves experiencing a cycle in which obscurities are progressively clarified; those clarifications are then reopened to new confusions that demand further clarifications of a sort that lend coherence (at a greater depth) to the experience of reading, and so on. The overall "shape" of dialectical movement is that of movement toward a never attained convergence of sets of meanings. And at the same time, reading early Bion includes a hefty dose of the experience of strange brilliance and brilliant strangeness – for example, his concept of beta-elements, alpha-function, the idea of being unable to fall asleep or wake up, and the application of mathematical concepts to psychoanalysis.

Bion's later work provides a markedly different experience in reading. If reading early Bion is an experience of movement toward convergence of disparate meanings, the experience of reading late Bion is an experience of movement toward an infinite expansion of meaning. In reading late Bion one must push oneself to one's limits, and then some, in an effort to sustain a state of active receptivity to every possible experience in reading. If reading early Bion is an experience of learning from experience, reading late Bion is an experience of disencumbering oneself of the deliberate use of all that one has learned from experience in order to be receptive to all that one does not know: "There is nothing more to be said about what you [the analyst] are prepared for; what you know, you know – we needn't bother with that. We have to deal with all that we don't know" (Bion, 1978, p. 149).

I will conclude this section of the chapter with two brief observations. First, it might be said that the reading of early Bion and the reading of late Bion are experiences that stand in dialectical tension with one another. But, on the basis of what I have discussed thus far, I believe that it is more accurate to describe the two experiences in reading as fundamentally different in nature. The two stand as different "vertices" (Bion, 1970, p. 93) from which to enter into an experience (whether it be an analytic experience with a patient or the reading of a text describing an analytic experience). They supplement one another as opposed to conversing with one another.

Second, in reading late Bion, it is important to bear in mind that O is not a philosophical, metaphysical, mathematical or theological conception; it is a psychoanalytic concept. Bion is exclusively interested in the psychoanalytic experience: he is concerned only with the analyst's task of overcoming what he knows in order to be at one with what is, the O of the analytic experience at any given moment. His conception of the analytic state of mind (reverie) is one in which the analyst makes himself as open as possible to experiencing what is true and attempts to find words to convey something of that truth to the patient. Transcendence of self on the part of the analyst is by no means an end in itself and is of no use whatever to the patient; the analyst's task is that of saying something "relatively truthful" (Bion, 1982, p. 8) regarding the emotional experience occurring at any given moment of the analysis which the patient might be able to use consciously and unconsciously for purposes of psychological growth.

A preface to an analytic experience

Before offering a clinical example illustrating the use in analytic practice of some of the ideas discussed above, it is necessary to introduce one additional concept (taken from Bion's late work) which, for me, represents a critical bridge between Bion's conception of the way the mind works and the experiential level of the psychoanalytic process. What I am referring to is a distinction that Bion makes in *Attention and Interpretation* between two types of remembering:

> We are familiar with the experience of *remembering* a dream; this must be contrasted with dreams that float into the mind unbidden *invited* and unsought and float away again as mysteriously. The emotional tone of this experience is not peculiar to the dream: thoughts also come unbidden, sharply, distinctly, with what appears to be unforgettable clarity, and then disappear leaving no trace by which they can be recaptured. I wish to reserve the term 'memory' for experience related to conscious attempts at recall. These [conscious attempts at recall] are expressions of a fear that some element, *become noticeable* 'uncertainties, mysteries, doubts', will obtrude.
>
> (1970, p. 70)
>
> *in an unwelcoming way*

For Bion, "memory" is an anxiety-driven use of the mind that interferes with the analyst's capacity to be receptive to what is true to the emotional experience, the O of that experience, as lived in the present moment. By contrast,

> Dream-like memory is the memory [memories that float into the mind unbidden] of psychic reality and is the stuff of analysis . . . the dream and the psycho-analyst's working material both share a dream-like quality.
>
> (ibid., pp. 70–71)

Thus, when the analyst is doing genuine analytic work, he is not "remembering," that is, not consciously attempting to know/understand/formulate the present by directing his attention to the past. Rather, he is experiencing the analysis in a "dream-like" way – he is dreaming the analytic session. An analyst consulting with Bion (1978) commented that she found his observations to be of such great value that she worried that she would not be able to remember them all. Bion replied that he hoped she would not remember anything of what he had said, but that it would make him happy if one day while in an analytic session, something of what had occurred in the consultation came back to her in a way that felt like an unexpected recollection of a dream and perhaps that dream-like remembering might be of help to her in saying something to the patient that he or she could make use of.

On not being "an analyst"

Mr. B, during a phone call in which we set up our first meeting, told me that he did not want analysis. In the initial session, he repeated his wish not to be in analysis and added that he had seen "the school shrink" while in college for a few sessions for insomnia, but could not remember the man's name. I chose not to ask for clarification of what Mr. B meant by "analysis" and why he was so set against it. My decision to desist from intervening in this way was based on a sense that to have done so would have been to ignore what this patient was trying very hard to tell me: he did not want me to be "an analyst" without a name, an analyst who conducted himself in a manner that represented the outcome of his experience with other patients. In my work with him, I was not to be who I thought I was or who I previously had been to any other person or to myself.

At the end of the first session, I suggested possible times to meet again later in the week. Mr. B opened his appointment book and told me which of the times would be best for him. I continued this method of arranging one future meeting at a time over the next several months; it seemed to suit Mr. B in that period of our work. In the course of the first several months, a schedule of daily meetings became established. In the second or third session, I told Mr. B that I thought I would be able to work best with him if he used the couch; we began working in that manner in the subsequent session. Mr. B told me that using the couch was a little strange, but it suited him too.

The patient at first said almost nothing about the present circumstances of his life, including how old he was. He mentioned his wife, but it was not clear how long they had been married, what sort of marriage it was or whether they had any children. I did not feel any inclination to inquire; his way of being with me, and my way of being with him, at that juncture seemed to be a more important form of communication than could be achieved through my making inquiries. When, on occasion, I did ask a question, the patient responded politely and earnestly, but the questions and responses seemed only to distract Mr. B and me from the task of introducing ourselves to one another at an unconscious level.

The "patient" – an odd word because Mr. B was not a patient in a way that was familiar to me – never told me why he had come to see me. I do not think he himself knew. Instead, he told me "stories" of events in his life that were important to him, but which did not "make a point" in the sense of illustrating a dilemma or describing a form of psychological pain concerning which he needed or wanted my help. I found his stories interesting: Mr. B regularly surprised me in that in his accounts he portrayed himself as a person who is just a little removed and a little "off" in an utterly unselfconscious (and endearing) way. For example, he told me that when he was in fourth grade, there was a new girl, L, in his class who had recently moved to the town in which he grew up. Her father had died the previous year, a fact that Mr. B found "riveting, mysterious and incomprehensible." He and L became very attached to one another; their relationship continued through the end of high school and into their first year of college. It was "very intense and very stormy."

An incident from this long relationship with L stood out in the patient's mind. The day after they had gone to a high school dance together, Mr. B went to L's house to pick her up for a drive that they had arranged. When the patient rang the doorbell, L's mother came to the door and told him that L was not home. Mr. B stood there for a moment, frozen with disbelief. He told me that he then got into his car and drove for hours, screaming in pain at the top of his lungs. Mr. B went on to say that L, years later, had told him that she had felt so embarrassed about having been hung over from drinking with some girlfriends after he had dropped her off that she had asked her mother to tell him that she was not at home.

In my interventions during the first year or so of the analysis, I used words very close to those used by the patient, but with the emphasis shifted just a bit. For instance, in response to the account of L's mother's having told Mr. B that L was not at home, I said, "How could you have known what was happening if you weren't being told the truth?" In speaking in this way, I was putting into words an idea and a set of feelings that addressed a good deal of what was happening in that phase of the analysis: I was underscoring the enormous importance to Mr. B of saying what is true. I took the story of L's mother's lie as an unconscious expression of the patient's feeling that I could hurt him deeply by not being truthful with him, by playing the role of analyst as opposed to being myself as *his* analyst. My comment to Mr. B was in part informed by a story he had told me months earlier: during a conversation that took place in a tenement, an albino cockroach scurried across Mr. B's notepad. The patient said in a matter-of-fact way that he had not been bothered by the cockroach: "Where else would a cockroach live if not in a tenement? I was the visitor, not him."

As Mr. B spoke of L's mother's lie, I wondered what I would do if one of my sons, during his high school years, had asked me to lie to one of his close friends. I could not imagine doing so, except under extraordinary circumstances. My mind wandered to a set of experiences with G, my best friend when we were ten or eleven years old. His family had moved to the United States from Australia only a couple of years earlier. I recalled G's habit of greatly exaggerating a story in his telling of it. When confronted with irrefutable evidence of his exaggeration, he would say, "I were only kidding." I was aware even as a child that G was using the word "were" instead of the word "was," and with that one exception, he said things the same way the rest of us did (albeit with an Australian accent). I found his habit of distorting the truth to be embarrassing in its desperateness. This was a particularly painful memory for me during the session with Mr. B because it was so closely linked with memories of my own acts of dishonesty in childhood which were still a source of shame for me. There had been a number of occasions when I had shown off to G's mother by mentioning a book I had read or a piece of national news I had heard about. I had not felt the need to posture in this way with the parents of any other of my friends. I remembered, too, how surprised I was that G called his mother by her first name. I emerged from this reverie with a deep sense of sadness for G, who had lived under such enormous pressure (both internal and external) to be someone he was not for his mother. Who he was — and who I was — was simply not good enough.

As my attention returned to Mr. B, he was telling me about riding his bicycle to school when he was about ten years old. He would stop periodically along the way and put a leaf or a stone or a bottle cap in a particular place — for example, between the boards of an old fence or in a cave that was "no more than a dug-out hole under a big rock." On the way home from school, he would retrieve these objects. Mr. B recalled with pleasure the feel of the wind on his face as he rode home on his bicycle and the feeling of amazement he felt that during the whole time that he was in school these things were there "spending the day doing something else" and were waiting for him on his way home. It seemed that the important thing about this childhood experience was the sense of security that Mr. B derived from knowing these things were alive (alive with meaning) just as he was alive in his own being at school. The carefully placed objects had an existence that went on in his absence: the stone and the leaf and the bottle cap went on being what they were. As Mr. B was telling me the story, the sound and cadences of his words reminded me of lines from a Borges (1957) prose poem: "All things long to persist in their being; the stone eternally wants to be a stone and the tiger a tiger" (p. 246).

In listening to Mr. B's story about the stones and leaves and bottle caps remaining themselves while he was at school (in conjunction with my reverie regarding G and his mother), it occurred to me that Mr. B had been frightened as a child – and now with me – that his connection with his mother (and me) felt thin, not based on truths that remain true, truths that can be taken utterly for granted, love that remains love, a mother who persists in her being as a mother *all the time*. I said to Mr. B, "It seems to me that you felt – although I don't know if you would put it this way – that L's mother was not being motherly either to L or to you in lying to you. There is something about being a mother that doesn't go together with lying. It's not a matter of ethics or sentimentality; it's a feeling that a mother, when she's being a mother, is telling the truth, she *is* the truth." Mr. B and I were silent for a few minutes until the end of the session.

Some months later, as Mr. B was beginning to be able to speak more directly about feelings, he told me that as a child, there were long stretches of time during which he felt frightened that he would come home and find that his mother had been taken over by aliens – she would no longer be his mother even though she looked exactly like his mother. He would try to devise questions, the answers to which only his real mother would know. He said, "I remember vividly that fear that I felt as a kid and only now recognize the loneliness that went with it. But at this moment, all I feel is cold – not distant or remote, but physically cold, as if the temperature in the room has suddenly dropped by 25 degrees."

Discussion

The work with Mr. B began with an unconscious request that I not be a generic analyst, and instead be a person capable of not knowing who I am and who he is. Only in that way would I be able to be open to what I do not know, i.e. to the O of who he is (and of who I am with him). If I was to be of any help to Mr. B, I would have to invent a psychoanalysis that bore his name, his being (in contrast to the therapy provided by his previous therapist, who had no name, i.e. who did not make a therapy with Mr. B that had their names on it).

Mr. B's unconscious request was a reasonable one – and every patient makes it – but for him, it held particular significance that derived from his own life experience including his relationship with his mother. Her state of being-his-mother felt not only unreliable, but untrue to him. In the early part of the analysis, this quality of his experience of his mother was brought to life in a great many forms. He unconsciously communicated to me through his unique way of being with me the importance to him of people being genuinely (truthfully) present with one another. He refused to adapt himself to what he imagined to be the prescribed form in which he was to take the role of a patient consulting a doctor concerning a malady for which he was seeking treatment. Rather, he seemed just to be there and I was to respond only to who he was. It was his being (the O of who he was) that I was to experience, not a pre-packaged substitute for O in the form of my preconceptions (or his) about analysis. My efforts to do so, for instance by setting up only one meeting at a time, did not feel like a contrivance, but rather as the way it had to be and should be with Mr. B at that point. I listened (with genuine interest) to his stories without trying to ferret out what the story was "really about"; the story was not *about* anything; the story was the story; O is O.

I attempted to speak to Mr. B in a way that emerged from what was true to the emotional experience that was occurring. In speaking of the lie that L's mother told the patient, I spoke of the confusion, the inability to think, in the face of a lie: "How could you have known what was happening if you weren't being told the truth?" Every interpretation that an analyst makes is directed to his own experience as well as that of the patient. In this instance, my interpretation served as a starting point for a reverie involving G's desperate exaggerations and my own feelings of shame concerning my own childhood emotional dishonesty (posturings). My feelings of shame were followed by sadness regarding G's (and my own) sense of inadequacy in the eyes of his mother. His ungrammatical use of the word "were" in his saying "I were only kidding," in retrospect, seems to have been a complex event reflecting the breakdown of language and thinking in the face of his own efforts to become a lie, i.e. to be someone other than who he was. Perhaps also the word "were" in his statement represented a strangulated beginning of a plea to his mother, a wish that she were a different kind of mother, a mother who could sincerely love him as he was, not as she wished he were.

Reverie, like dreaming, while often involving great complexity of feeling, is nonetheless a form of unmediated or barely mediated experience. In reveries and dreams there is almost nothing of a reflective self. Even when an apparently observing self is a figure in a dream, that figure has no greater powers of observation than any other figure in the dream (including the narrator). In this sense, I view reverie as an *experience of what is* at an unconscious level in the analytic relationship – the O of the unconscious of the analyst and analysand living in the experience of the unconscious analytic third (Ogden, 1994a, 1994b, 1999). The reverie concerning my friend G and his mother was not *about* the unconscious events occurring in the analysis at that point – it *was* the O of the unconscious experience at that point.

Mr. B's response to my interpretation concerning his inability to know what was happening in the face of a lie took the form of his telling me a story about his way of reassuring himself as a child that things (and, by extension, people) remain true to who they are when out of sight. (As time went on, the patient's stories became more layered with meaning, for example, as reflected in the way the story of the hidden stones and leaves lent itself more naturally to verbally symbolic interpretation.)

I spoke to Mr. B in terms of the feelings and images that he had introduced (and in terms of feelings that I had experienced in my reverie). I told him that I thought he felt that L's mother had not been a mother to L or to him in lying to him and that being a mother is somehow *to be* what is true. Of course, I was also saying indirectly that being an analyst is somehow to be what is true, i.e. that it is my job to attempt to become and say the truth, the O of the emotional experience at a given juncture of the analysis. (The knowledge that the analyst cannot possibly succeed in this effort to say and be what is true was addressed by Bion in response to the self-criticism of an analyst who was presenting a session to him. The analyst was chastising herself for the inadequacy of her interpretations. Bion, nearly

80 at the time, commented: "If you had been practising analysis as long as I have, you wouldn't bother about an inadequate interpretation – I have never given any other kind. That is real life – not psycho-analytic fiction" [1975, p. 43].)

It seems fitting to conclude this chapter with a mention of Mr. B's comments about his childhood fear that he would find that his mother was no longer really his mother. His experience in the analysis at that juncture captures something of the difference between, on the one hand, remembering an experience (his recollecting his childhood fear and loneliness), and on the other, becoming the O of the experience (his feeling chilled, his becoming that chilling experience).

7

Elements of analytic style

Bion's clinical seminars

For some years now, it has seemed to me that important aspects of my way of practising psychoanalysis are better described as an analytic style than as an analytic technique. Though style and technique are inseparable, for the purposes of the present discussion, I will use the term *analytic technique* to refer to a way of practising analysis that has been, to a large extent, developed by a branch or group of branches of one's analytic ancestry, as opposed to being a creation of one's own. By contrast, *analytic style* is not a set of principles of practice, but a living process that has its origins in the personality and experience of the analyst.

The term *analytic style*, as I am using it, puts equal emphasis on the word *analytic* as on the word *style*. Not every style that an analyst may adopt is analytic, and not every way of practising psychoanalysis bears the unique mark (the "style") of the analyst. The idea of analytic style places greater emphasis than does the concept of analytic technique on the role of (1) the analyst's use of, and capacity to speak from, the unique qualities of his personality; (2) the analyst's making use of his own experience as analyst, analysand, parent, child, spouse, teacher, student, friend and so on; (3) the analyst's ability to think in a way that draws on, but is independent of, the analytic theory and clinical technique of his analyst, supervisors, analytic colleagues and analytic ancestors; the analyst must learn analytic theory and technique so thoroughly that one day he will be able to forget them (Ogden, 2005a); and (4) the responsibility of the analyst to invent psychoanalysis freshly with each patient (Ogden, 2004a).

The analyst's style is a living, ever-changing way of being with himself and the patient. The entirety of the analyst's style is present in every session with every patient; and yet, particular elements of his style play a greater role than others with any given patient in any given session. Analytic style infuses the specific ways the analyst conducts himself in the analysis. Style shapes and colors method, and method is the medium in which style comes to life.

My thinking about analytic style has been strongly influenced by Bion's work. Of all of Bion's published contributions, the "Clinical seminars" (1987), for me, provide the richest and most extensive access available to Bion the clinician. In the present chapter, I will offer close readings of three of the clinical seminars. I will describe what I view as Bion's unique analytic style, and in so doing illustrate what I mean by the idea of analytic style.

In the decade between the publication of his last major psycho-analytic work, *Attention and Interpretation* (1970), and his death in 1979, Bion conducted two series of clinical seminars: 24 in Brasilia in 1975, and 28 in São Paulo in 1978. In these seminars, in addition to the analyst who presented a case to Bion, there were six or seven other seminar members, as well as a translator. The seminars were tape recorded, but it was not until 1987 that the collected, transcribed and edited version was published. I believe that despite the fact that in the seminars Bion is the supervisor and group leader, the "Clinical seminars" nonetheless afford the reader a rare opportunity to view Bion, the clinician, at work. As will be seen, even though Bion is not the analyst for the presenter's patient, he is the analyst for the patient being "dreamt up" in the clinical seminar. (I have previously discussed the idea that the patient presented in analytic supervision is "a fiction," an imaginary patient dreamt up by analyst and supervisor, as opposed to the actual person with whom the analyst converses in his consulting room [Ogden, 2005a, 2006].) In addition, in the clinical seminars, Bion does analytic work both with the presenter and with the seminar group.

Three clinical seminars

A patient who feared what the analyst might do (Brasilia, 1975, Seminar No. 1)

The seminar opens with the following exchange:

Presenter: I would like to discuss a session I had today with a thirty-year-old woman. She came into the consulting room and sat down; she never lies on the couch. She smiled and said, "Today I won't be able to stay sitting here." I asked her what that meant; she said she was very agitated. I asked her what she considered as being very agitated. She smiled and said, "My head is dizzy." She said her thoughts were running away, running over one another. I suggested that when she felt like that she also felt that she was losing control of her body. She smiled and said, "Perhaps; it looks as if that were true." When I continued, suggesting that when her mind was running away like that, her body had to follow her mind's movements, she interrupted me, saying, "Now, don't you try to make me stand still."

Bion: Why should this patient think that the analyst would *do* anything? You cannot stop her coming or send her away; she is a grown woman and presumably therefore free to come and see you if she wants to; if she doesn't want to, she is free to go away. Why does she say that you would try to stop her doing something? I am not really asking for an answer to that question – although I would be very glad to hear any answer that you have – but simply giving an example of what my reaction is to this story.

(Bion, 1987, pp. 3–4)

[Unless otherwise indicated, all subsequent page numbers cited refer to Bion, 1987, "Clinical seminars"]

Bion inquires, "Why should this patient think that the analyst would *do* anything?" This question to the presenter is, for me, quite startling and more than a bit odd. Of the innumerable aspects of the clinical material presented, why is Bion asking about why the patient would think that the analyst would take action? Only after

119

considerable reflection did it occur to me that Bion is suggesting that the presenter ask himself: What kind of thinking is the patient engaging in? Why is she thinking in this particular way? Bion is drawing attention to the fact that the patient is engaged in a very limited sort of thinking in which elements of experience that might (under other circumstances) be transformed into thoughts and feelings, in this instance are being experienced and expressed in the medium of action. The analyst's thoughts are being treated as actions (active forces emanating from the analyst) that hold the power to get the patient to do (not think) something. So the question, "Why should the patient think that the analyst would *do* anything?" is, at its core, a question concerning the way in which the patient is attempting to handle the emotional problem of the moment, and, perhaps, of the entire session: her fear that she is losing her mind.

The patient's evacuation of her unthinkable thought (her fear that she is going mad) has precipitated a rift with external reality in the form of the delusional belief that the analyst is trying to do something to her, i.e. "to make me stand still." If the analyst is too frightened to take seriously the patient's statement that she believes in a very concrete way that he is trying to *do* something to her, he will compound the patient's problems by failing to think/dream (to do conscious and unconscious psychological work with) the patient's delusional experience (Bion, 1962a).

Bion, in "simply giving an example of what my reaction is to this story," is giving an unobtrusive interpretation to the presenter. The presenter offered the patient a verbally symbolized thought that he hoped would help her to think about her own experience: "I suggested that when she felt like that [i.e. that her thoughts were running over one another] she also felt that she was losing control of her body." The patient responded by smiling and saying, "Perhaps; it looks as if that were true." Her smile (the mention of which has a chilling effect on me) is followed by a statement that seems to offer qualified ("Perhaps") agreement. But the words, "it looks as if that were true," in combination with her smile, seem to me to convey the idea that the analyst sees only what *appears* to be true, and not what is in fact true to what the patient is experiencing. .

The analyst ignored the patient's response and repeated his interpretation. The patient interrupted the analyst's repetition of his interpretation by saying, "Now, don't you try to make me stand still." She might as well have said, "Stop doing that to me. Stop trying to make me into you by putting your ideas into my head and in that way controlling my actions (making me stand still). If that happens, I won't be able to move my own mind and body at all." In asking why the patient would think that the analyst would *do* anything, Bion is, I believe, trying to help the presenter to understand this aspect of the patient's psychotic thinking.

The presenter responds at a superficial level to Bion's question – "Why should the patient think that the analyst would *do* anything?" – by saying,

> I was interested to know why she had said "Don't try to keep me still". She said she didn't know the answer to the question, so I suggested that she was preoccupied by my being quiet, still. She said that she did not regard me as being still, but as dominating my movements, my mind controlling my body.
>
> (p. 4)

The presenter's inability to use Bion's question/interpretation reflected, I believe, his fear of recognizing (thinking) the full extent of his patient's psychosis. Because the patient cannot differentiate mind from body (and herself from the analyst), her saying that she experienced his mind as dominating his body was, I believe, equivalent to her saying that she experienced *his* mind as dominating *her* body and mind. In other words, he was relentless in his effort to get into her mind and make her *do* things ("make me stand still" mentally and physically).

Bion told the seminar,

> I would like to make a guess here as to what I would say to this patient – not in the first session but later on. "We have here these chairs, this couch, because you might want to use any of them; you might want to sit in that chair, or you might want to lie on that couch in case you feel that you couldn't bear sitting there – as you say today. That is why this couch was here when you first came. I wonder what has made you discover this today. Why is it only today you have found that you may not be able to sit in that chair; that you may have to lie down or go away?" All that would be much more appropriate if she had discovered it at the first session. But she was too afraid to discover it.
>
> (pp. 4–5)

This, at first, seems like a very strange thing to say. But I view it as a reflection of Bion's analytic style. Only Bion could have said this. If someone else were to say this, he would be imitating Bion. So what is Bion doing here, or, to put it in different terms, how is Bion being Bion-the-analyst here? He is treating the encounter as if it were the first encounter between him and the patient. He recognizes that the patient is predominantly psychotic and speaks to her from that vantage point (thereby recognizing who she is at that moment). For Bion (1957), the psychotic aspect of the personality is a part of the self that is unable to think, to learn from experience or do psychological work.

Speaking to "the non-psychotic part of the patient's personality" (Bion, 1957), the part capable of thinking and doing psychological work, Bion begins by naming in the simplest, most literal terms the objects that are in the consulting room (which are swirling with uncontrolled meaning for the patient because she is frightened and unable to think): "We have here these chairs, this couch, because you might want to use any of them." Bion, in this way, not only tells the patient what the objects are – as external objects – he also tells her implicitly that they are there for her to use as analytic objects, objects that may be used in dreaming up an analysis, if she wishes to try to do so (with his help). He continues: "you might want to sit in that chair, or you might want to lie on that couch in case you feel that you couldn't bear sitting there – as you say today." Here, Bion tells the patient that he thinks that she may be frightened of using the chair today. I believe that Bion is implicitly speculating imaginatively that the chair, for the patient, is a psychological place that once held magical power to protect her against what she fears would happen if she "really" were in analysis. The chair, for some reason, has lost its power today. She might want to use the couch (i.e. she may want to try to become the analytic patient who she had hoped to become when she first came to see the analyst). Bion is not trying to do something to her or to get her to do something, for example, to use the chair or the couch; he is attempting to help her to "dream herself into existence" (Ogden, 2004a) as an analysand and dream him up as an analyst who may be able to help her to think: "That is why the couch was here when you first came."

Bion, in a way that is characteristic of him in the "Clinical seminars," frames his inquiry in the form of the question, "I wonder what has made you discover this today?" i.e. how have you discovered that this is the emotional problem that is most important for you to solve in today's session? He is implicitly adding that *he* does not have a solution to the problem, but that *she* may, and that he may be able to help her to understand something of the problem that is disturbing her, but which she, as yet, is unable to think/dream. Further, what Bion is implicitly saying might be phrased as follows: "In your saying, 'Today I won't be able to stay sitting here,' you are telling me that you are afraid that you can no longer get help here – you fear that you have become so mad ('dizzy') that you have lost hope of being able to become a patient who may be able to make use of me as your analyst."

Bion continues to wonder aloud: "[So] why is it that only today you have found that you may not be able to sit in that chair; that you may have to lie down or go away?" Bion's interpretation (ostensibly to the patient) is perhaps more an interpretation to the presenter: the presenter had not recognized or spoken to the patient about her fear of not being able to be a patient in analysis, a fear she expressed both in her stated inability to use either the chair or the couch and in her statement that the analyst seems to the patient to be able to perceive only what "looks as if . . . [it] were true." It now seems clearer to me why I find the patient's smile so chilling: it bespeaks the enormity of the emotional disconnection that the patient was experiencing between the degree of her emotional distress and her very limited ability to think/dream it, and between herself and the analyst.

Not long after making this interpretation to the patient (and also to the presenter), Bion says, "As the analyst, one hopes to go on improving – as well as the patient . . . If I knew all the answers I would have nothing to learn, no chance of learning anything . . . What one wants is to have room to live as a human being who makes mistakes" (p. 6). This, too, is a fundamental element of Bion's style in the "Clinical seminars." Though time and again, Bion surprises the presenter and the reader with his uncanny way of sensing the importance of, and making analytic use of, seemingly insignificant elements of what is happening in a session, he no less frequently states, without contrived humility, that an analyst must "have room to live as a human being who makes mistakes." Only in this state of mind is one able to learn from experience: "If you had been prac-tising analysis as long as I have, you wouldn't bother about an inad-equate interpretation – I have never given any other kind. That is real life – not psycho-analytic fiction" (p. 49).

123

Before turning to the next seminar, there is an implicit element of Bion's clinical approach in this seminar and in a great many others to which I would like to draw the reader's attention: the question that Bion asks the presenting analyst far more often than he asks any other question is: Why is the patient coming to analysis? (see, for example, pp. 20, 41, 47, 76, 102, 143, 168, 183, 187, 200, 225 and 234). It seems to me that in each instance that Bion poses this question, he is implicitly asking the presenter to think of the patient as unconsciously bringing to each session an emotional problem for which he has been unable to find a "solution" (p. 100), i.e. a problem with which he has been unable to do psychological work. The patient is unconsciously asking the analyst to help him to think the disturbing thoughts and feelings that he is unable to think and feel on his own. Though Bion, in the seminar just discussed, does not explicitly ask the presenter why the patient is coming to analysis, it seems to me that he implicitly raises that question several times. The first instance occurs almost immediately in the seminar when he says, "she is a grown woman and therefore presumably free to come and see you if she wants to; if she doesn't want to, she is free to go away."

A doctor who was not himself (Brasilia, 1975, Seminar No. 3)

This seminar is quite remarkable in the way that it generates a conversation which affords Bion the opportunity not only to put into words, but to demonstrate so much of his conception of what it means to be an analyst. What is more, Bion does so without using a single technical term. This is consonant with his insistence that we speak to our patients in "words that are as simple and unmistakable as possible" (p. 234), in everyday language, "ordinary articulate speech" (p. 144), and that we, as analysts, talk to one another in the same way.

The analysand being presented is a 24-year-old hospital physician who has been unable to work for four months. He told the analyst, "I took the elevator not feeling well. I thought it would be too difficult to come to the session. I thought that if I stayed here I would die" (p. 13). The presenter said that the patient then changed the subject and began to describe his attempt to return to work the previous day despite intense anxiety.

Bion asked, "Was he physically ill?" (p. 13). Once again, Bion's question seems odd, this time because it seems so literal-minded.

(There is something surprisingly pragmatic about Bion's way of listening to the presenters' accounts of their work with their patients throughout the "Clinical seminars.") Perhaps in asking whether the patient was physically ill, Bion is pointing out that the patient, even though he says that he was afraid that he was dying, has come to see an analyst, not a doctor of internal medicine. It must be that his experience to this point in analysis has led him to feel that the analyst has helped him and that he and the analysis may be of further help to him.

The presenter responds only to the most superficial level of Bion's question by saying, "He thought so [i.e. the patient was consciously aware only of feeling physically ill] but in fact he was suffering an anxiety crisis" (p. 13). Bion is unfazed by the presenter's inability to understand the observation that was implicit in his question. This event, though of no great significance in itself, reflects a critical quality of Bion's style as a supervisor and (I surmise) as an analyst: he "speaks past the presenter." That is, he speaks to that aspect of the presenter that is able to think – the thinking aspect of the personality, which Bion, in his theoretical writings, at times calls "the non-psychotic part of the personality," and at other times, "the unconscious." It is this aspect of the personality that is capable of making use of lived experience for purposes of psychological work and growth. I will use the terms "speaking past the patient," "speaking to the unconscious" and "speaking to the non-psychotic part of the personality" interchangeably in referring to the analyst's act of speaking to the aspect of the patient that is capable of thinking. Since the conscious aspect of the presenter's mind is, in the instance being discussed, not fully able to think, Bion must speak "directly" to the patient's unconscious or non-psychotic aspect of personality (see Grotstein, 2007a, 2007b, for discussions of talking to the patient's unconscious).

A member of the seminar then asks whether it might "not be interesting to interrupt the patient at this point? I feel there is too much material" (p. 14). Bion responds by saying that he would wait to say something until he had "a clearer idea of what he [the patient] was up to" (p.14). He adds,

it's just a suspicion working in my mind – that this patient is one of those people who take up medicine because they are so frightened of some catastrophe or disaster. He can then converse with other doctors and thereby hear about all the diseases there are.

125

Then he won't die, or disasters won't happen, because he is the
doctor, not the patient.

(p. 14)

The patient, even though he has qualified as a doctor, is not a doctor
because he has no idea about how to genuinely become a doctor, i.e.
how to develop a sense of coming into being as a person who is able
to use his mind to help people (including himself) who are ill.

The same seminar member repeated his question in a slightly
different form: "Is this suspicion of yours one of those things the
analyst should keep to himself, or could he tell the patient?" (p. 14).
Bion makes an interpretation meant for this seminar member, but
couched as a statement concerning the patient. He tells the seminar
member that people can only do psychological work with a bit of
their lived experience and, in particular, analysts early in their career
often feel deluged by frightening experiences with their patients:

A common manifestation of this sort of thing happens when
medical students go to the dissecting room to learn anatomy. They
break down; they can't go on with it because it causes such an
upheaval in their views and attitudes if they dissect the human
body.

(p. 14)

Bion, I believe, is saying that he suspects that the seminar member
feels compelled to interrupt the flow of thinking (dissecting) in the
seminar for fear of breaking down in the analytic "dissecting room"
(the clinical seminar). Bion's style of interpretation is highly respectful
of the seminar member's defenses as well as his dignity. The thinking
that Bion is offering is there to be used if and when the seminar
member is ready to make use of it. Without shaming the seminar
member, the interpretation seems to have been utilizable by him –
his unconscious fear of what he might find out in the seminar was
diminished to the point that he was able not to make further inter-
ruptions of the analytic work that was occurring in the seminar.

Immediately following Bion's response to the seminar member
just described, the presenter said, "I have the feeling that the
patient didn't change the subject – he only apparently changed it"
(p. 14). Here the presenter is contradicting his own statement made
only a few moments earlier. I surmise that in the interim he made

126

psychological use of the interpretation that Bion made to the seminar member, i.e. that the analyst's anxiety may prevent him from listening to what the patient is unconsciously trying to communicate regarding his fears.

Bion replies to the presenter:

> This feeling of yours is where the interpretation comes from . . . When you begin to feel that all these different free associations are not really different ones, because they have the same pattern, then it becomes important to wait until you know what the pattern is.
>
> (p. 14)

The presenter responds:

> In a seminar with a training analyst, the analyst told me that every good interpretation should contain three elements: a description of the behaviour of the patient; the function of the behaviour; and the theory which is behind the behaviour.
>
> (p. 15)

The reader can almost feel Bion's blood coming to a boil – not in response to the presenter's anxiety, but in response to the arrogance of an analyst who believes that he knows how to do psychoanalysis, and believes that if his supervisees see things as he does, they, too, will know how to do psychoanalysis. Nevertheless, Bion's response is a measured one, but not completely bleached of his feeling that a supervisory style of the sort described is destructive to the supervisee's efforts to become an analyst. At the same time, Bion is fully aware that he is not hearing the ideas of the training analyst (about whom Bion knows nothing), but the ideas and feelings of the presenter who, like his own patient, has momentarily retreated from being a thinking doctor (an analyst) into a passive patient who cannot think for himself. Bion says:

> In a sense these theories, such as the one you mention, have a use for the particular person who mentions them. [Bion does not identify that person as the training analyst because he is not addressing that person. He is addressing a split in the presenter's personality in which one aspect of himself – who uses analytic theory as a way of not thinking – belittles another aspect of himself

127

– who is trying to become a thinking analyst.] Some of them [analytic theories] will also mean something to you. [The thinking aspect of the presenter may, at times, be able to think about analytic theories and find them useful to him in developing his own ideas.] While you are trying to learn, all these things are very confusing. [Being confused is a state of mind to be experienced as opposed to being evacuated and replaced by a feeling that one knows how to do analysis because one has been told how to do so by someone in authority.] This is why I think you can [Bion does not say, "one can"] go on too long with training and seminars. It is only *after* you have qualified [as an analyst] that you have a chance of becoming an analyst. The analyst you become is you and you alone; you have to respect the uniqueness of your own personality – that is what you use, not all these interpretations [these theories that you use to combat the fear that you are not really an analyst and do not know how to become one].

(p. 15)

Bion is demonstrating for the presenter, the seminar members, and the reader what a genuine analytic conversation sounds like. Interpretations do not announce themselves as interpretations. They are a part of "a conversation" (p. 156) in which ideas are stated tactfully, respectfully (often as conjectures) in everyday language. It is becoming clear here that what Bion means by interpretation is not a statement designed to provide verbal symbolization for repressed unconscious conflict in an effort to make the unconscious conscious. Rather, an interpretation is a way of telling the patient a portion of what the analyst is thinking in a form that the patient may be able to use in thinking his own thoughts.

The reader of this seminar can hear with his or her own ears what a person who is able to speak from the uniqueness of his personality and experience sounds like. No other analyst sounds remotely like Bion. In the other chapters of this book I discuss the unique ways in which other major analytic writers speak/write/think in a way that reflects the uniqueness of his or her personality. It would be very difficult, even in reading a short passage, not to recognize the distinctive voice of each of these analysts.

The analyst's ability to speak with humility from the uniqueness of his personality, from his own "peculiar mentality" (p. 224), lies at the core of what I am calling the analyst's style. It must be apparent by this time that style is the opposite of fashion; it is also the opposite of narcissism. Giving oneself over to fashion arises from the wish to be like others (in the absence of a sense of who one is); narcissism involves a wish to be admired by others (in an effort to combat one's sense of worthlessness).

Following this "digression" in which Bion discusses the difficulties inherent in becoming an analyst, he asks the presenter to tell him more about the session:

Presenter: The patient had the impression that if he remained on duty [as a doctor at the hospital the previous night] he was going to feel ill. He was not feeling ill – he had the impression that this was going to happen.

Bion: In other words, he wasn't going to get cured – he would get these illnesses. It sounds possible that he has never really considered that he has to be very tough indeed to be a doctor at all. In this profession you are always dealing with people at their worst; they are frightened; they are anxious. It is no good taking up that occupation if he is going to end up by being anxious, depressed and frightened too.

(pp. 16–17)

Bion is making an indirect interpretation to the non-psychotic aspect of the presenter's personality. Here again, the interpretation has a surprisingly pragmatic feel to it: the patient has chosen a career for which he is not emotionally equipped – he seems not to be able to face other people's fears without becoming frightened and depressed himself. But, of course, there is more to the interpretation than that. Bion is focusing on a striking contradiction that seems to provide a sense of the nature of the emotional problem for which the patient is seeking help in this session. Why is the patient presenting the analyst with a contradiction in *this* particular way, at *this* moment? Perhaps the patient did not simply make a poor career choice. Is there something about himself (an aspect of himself that *is* a genuine doctor) from whom the patient feels disconnected? Bion is noticing a communication that is so obvious that it is as invisible as Poe's purloined letter. Perhaps it is this paradox – that the obvious is invisible – that makes Bion's comments sound odd and concrete. Here, as was the case earlier in the seminar, Bion's observation concerning something that feels "off" to him contains an "imaginative conjecture" (p. 191) regarding the emotional problem that the patient (with the analyst's help) is attempting to "solve" (p. 125), i.e. to think in this session. The question is not simply, "What is leading the patient to feel anxious and fearful?" A more specific problem (or facet of the dynamic tension driving the patient's symptomatology) is alive in the current session. Bion, in his comments that address the patient's choice of profession, seems to be trying out the idea that the patient may feel that *he is not himself*. He chose to try to become a doctor, and yet he feels more drawn to being a passive patient – a person who knows nothing, and wishes to know nothing, about the illness from which he is suffering.

Bion's speculation might be thought of as an interpretation spoken to the non-psychotic aspect of his "imaginary" patient, an aspect of personality that is both unconscious and capable of thinking.

The presenter seems to have been able to make use of this interpretation:

> So he left the room to lie down. At this moment he was called to the emergency ward. He went; he worked perfectly. He thought it very curious that he could work well without any difficulty.
>
> (p. 17)

It might be argued that the presenter's account of "what happened next" constitutes a mere recitation of notes that he had written days or weeks earlier. I find this idea unconvincing. The presenter could have said anything in response to Bion's "interpretation": for example, he could have asked a question that would have disrupted analytic thinking in the seminar or he could have made distracting comments about the patient's conscious reasons for seeking medical training. What the presenter did say involved an unintended, highly meaningful ambiguity: the word *curious* is a euphemism for the patient's feeling at a loss to account for what happened; and at the same time the word *curious* refers to the beginning of the capacity for thinking (the capacity to be curious about what one does not know). The former is a much more passive state of mind than the latter. In his use of the word *curious*, the presenter conveyed his growing understanding of the way in which the patient simultaneously wished to think and was afraid to think.

Bion responds by saying, "He goes off to this emergency, and instead of having a heart attack or whatever, he finds that he can be a doctor" (p. 17). The patient, with the analyst's help, is finding that he is able to become a doctor, i.e. a person who is able to think and to use that capacity to "dream himself into existence" as a doctor and as an analytic patient. Similarly, with the help of Bion's interpretations, the presenter is able to dream himself into existence as a doctor, i.e. as an analyst. He is becoming able to be curious about the patient, a person "at his worst" (a person who is anxious and in dire need of help).

To return to Bion's response to the patient's unexpectedly becoming a genuine doctor, Bion observes,

> Using this [event in which the patient became a doctor] not only for this incident but for many others, you can begin to feel that the patient may after all be a doctor or a potential analyst if, when it comes to a crisis, the doctor emerges. But why in a crisis? If it is really true that he may after all be a doctor, not just by title but the thing itself, why hasn't he discovered that until now? ... Of course, we believe as analysts – rightly or wrongly – that analysis is helpful. But this belief is liable to hide from us the extraordinary nature, the mystery of psychoanalysis. Such a lot of analysts seem to be bored with their subject; they have lost the capacity for wonder.
>
> (p. 17)

Two critical elements of Bion's style are audible in these sentences. First, we hear Bion, the doctor, the pragmatist, a person for whom finding "the solution to [the patient's] problem" (p. 100) matters greatly. Bion views his responsibility to be that of helping patients – a rather old-fashioned idea. If we do not believe that analysis is helpful, why are we spending our lives practising it? How are we to ignore the patient's pain, for it is his pain that leads him to seek help from the analyst? But it does not follow that the analyst's job is to help relieve the patient of pain. Quite the opposite. The analyst's task, for Bion, is to help the patient to live with his pain long enough to do analytic work with it. There is some aspect of the patient that comes to the analyst for analysis. Bion is continually listening for the (often very muted) voice of that part of the patient and for hints from the patient concerning what emotional problem this aspect of the patient is trying to think/solve. If the patient is not using the analyst as an analyst (for example by behaving as if he expects the analyst to be a magician whom will turn the patient into the person who he wishes to be), Bion asks himself (and often asks the "dreamt-up" patient) what the patient thinks analysts do. Perhaps second only in frequency to Bion's question, "Why has the patient come for analysis?" is his question, "What does the patient think analysis is?" And he often comments in response to the patient's idea, "That is a very strange conception of analysis." Helping the patient and giving the patient the "correct" (p. 162) analysis (a genuine analytic experience) are, for Bion, one and the same thing.

The second important element of Bion's analytic style that is alive in this passage is his feeling that his awareness of how little he knows is not a source of frustration or disappointment; it is a source of awe and wonderment in the face of the complexity, the beauty, and the horror that constitute human nature and human efforts to cope with and learn from disturbing experience. (See Gabbard, 2007, for a discussion of the role of analytic orthodoxy and the use of analytic dogma to evade facing the full complexity and "chaos of the human condition" [p. 35] and of the analytic enterprise.)

In response to the questions and associations that were elicited in Bion by the patient's having begun to develop his capacity for thinking, the presenter continues:

> Later on in the same session he [the patient] asked himself this question [How did he manage to genuinely become a doctor?] and said, "If I had known that analysis could do this for me I wouldn't have waited for a crisis before coming."

cehirigym attaque
                                                              (p. 17)

The reader can hear in this comment a shift in the balance of power between the patient as an assailant of his own capacity for thinking, and the patient as a thinking doctor. The doctor is now able to face the fact that he is ill while remaining alive to his feelings; he is able to make use of his awareness of his emotions to give direction to his thinking; and he is able to use his thinking to become "an analyst" who actively takes responsibility for his role in his own analysis.

Bion recognizes that the satisfaction to be taken by the patient in this achievement is balanced by feelings of sadness that are equally intense: "One of the peculiarities of progress is that it always makes you feel depressed or regretful that you didn't discover it sooner" (p. 17). This interpretation is meant not only for the imaginary patient being dreamt up in the seminar, but also for the presenter who, I think, Bion feels is regretful that it has taken him so long to become an analyst for his patient. (Perhaps the presenter recognized in the course of the seminar that he had relied for a long time on the thinking of others – the "training analyst" in himself – who had been afraid to respond freshly, without preconception, to what he was perceiving and feeling in the analytic sessions. In other words, to this point he had been unable to invent/rediscover psychoanalysis with this patient.

Still another element of Bion's analytic style can be felt in this portion of the seminar. As we have seen, Bion is continually aware of the way in which each patient in each analytic hour unconsciously feels that his life is at stake (and, it seems to me, that Bion believes, in an important sense, that the patient is correct in believing so). After all, to the extent that a patient cannot think, he cannot be alive to his experience. But Bion, here, takes a more radical position than he took earlier regarding the analyst's use of himself in his effort to help the patient. What he adds is critical to who Bion is as an analyst:

> You are an analyst, or a father or a mother, because you believe you are capable of the affection or understanding which is so necessary but which is felt [by the patient and the child] to be so unimportant [i.e. it is invisible to them because it is completely taken for granted, as it should be] . . . It is liable to be lost sight of that what we, as doctors and psycho-analysts, are concerned with is helping human beings . . . We may have to upset them in the course of the analysis, but that is not what we are trying to do. With this patient it may be very important to show him, when the time comes, that there exists [in the analyst] some capacity for affection, sympathy, understanding – not just diagnoses [interpretations] and surgery, not just analytic jargon, but interest in the person. You can't make doctors or analysts – they have to be born.
>
> (p. 18)

Bion, in his characteristically understated way, is saying that, for him, being an analyst involves more than understanding the patient and communicating to him that understanding in a form that he can make use of; being an analyst involves, at times, feeling *and showing* one's affection for the patient about whom the analyst cares deeply.

This is something that one cannot be taught to do; one must be born with a capacity to do it, and a wish to do it.

A man who was perpetually awake
(Sâo Paulo, 1978, Seminar No. 1)

In this seminar, the patient being presented is a 38-year-old econo-mist who has a rather mechanical walk and conducts himself in a stiff manner, for example, by opening a session by saying, "Very well, Doctor," or "I have brought you some dreams today" (p. 141).

Bion very soon asks another of his "odd" questions: "Why does he say they are dreams?" (p. 142). Bion is immediately cutting to the core of what he believes is the emotional problem with which the patient is unconsciously asking for help from the analyst: the non-psychotic aspect of the patient recognizes that the psychotic aspect of himself is dominating his personality and consequently he cannot dream. Bion is suggesting with his question that to the extent that the patient is psychotic, he cannot differentiate dreaming from waking perception, i.e. he cannot tell whether he is asleep or awake. For Bion (1962a), the psychotic patient (or aspect of the patient) is unable to generate and maintain a barrier (the "contact-barrier," p. 21) between conscious and unconscious aspects of mind. In the absence of differentiation between conscious and unconscious mental experi-ence, the individual "cannot go to sleep and cannot wake up" (p. 7). He lives in a world in which internally generated perception (hallu-cination) is undifferentiable both from perception of external events and from dreaming. Consequently, the patient (in order to protect himself from this frightening awareness) pretends to be a person who is interested in dreams.

The presenter, like the reader, has not thought to ask himself why the patient says he had dreams, what the patient means when he speaks of having had dreams, and whether or not the patient, at this moment, knows what a dream is. Nonplussed by Bion's question, "Why does he say they are dreams?" the presenter replies, "He simply tells me so" (p. 142).

The element of Bion's analytic style to which I am drawing atten-tion here is his extraordinarily quick wit. In this exchange, he is casting the presenter as a straight man in a magic show in which Bion pulls a rabbit out of the presenter's vest pocket. Bion is perfectly straight-faced throughout. Wit is neither an inherently good nor bad quality of character. How it is used is what matters. At 80, Bion is, in this instance, playing the role of enigmatic, idiosyncratic, unpredictable, razor-sharp old man – a role that seems to suit him. Another example of Bion's wit that comes to mind is a comment he made in Brasilia Seminar No. 8. The presenter told Bion that the patient had said he had managed to control his envy, but kept moving anxiously on the couch throughout the session. Bion replied, "He controlled envy and his envy is extremely annoyed about it" (p. 48).

It is never easy – perhaps it is impossible – to "read" Bion (i.e. to say with certainty who he "really is" at a given moment). He is a thoughtful, earnest teacher, fully aware of the limits of his knowledge and of his personality; and at the same time, he is a man who means what he says, and a man who invites (and helps) students and patients to do the same. There is also a reticence to Bion in the "Clinical seminars." His wit and enigmatic statements are part, I believe, of an effort to safeguard the sanctity of his privacy. This, too, is an integral part of Bion's analytic style, an integral part of who Bion is as an analyst and as a person.

A few moments later in the seminar, Bion speaks at greater length about the question that the patient was raising in his mind:

So why does the patient come to see a psycho-analyst and say he had a dream? I can imagine myself saying to a patient, "Where were you last night? What did you see?" If the patient told me he didn't see anything – he just went to bed – I would say, "Well, I still want to know where you went and what you saw."

(p. 142)

Bion, in this way, is saying to the non-psychotic part of the patient's personality that he understands that the patient does not know when he is awake and when he is asleep. So when the patient tells him that he went to bed, Bion treats the "dream" as an experience that has all the qualities of waking-life experience. Bion continues: "If the patient said, 'Ah, well, I had a dream', then I would want to know why he says it was a dream" (p. 142). By not accepting the patient's use of the word *dream* (which serves to evade the truth), Bion is helping the non-psychotic aspect of the patient's personality to think (which involves facing the reality of the current hegemony of the psychotic aspect of his personality). Bion is

135

implicitly stating his belief that such recognition of the truth of what is occurring influences the balance of power between the psychotic and the non-psychotic aspects of the personality.

Bion, shortly after, elaborates on this idea:

> when he says that [he had a dream], he is awake and 'conscious', as we call it. So – both the patient and you [the presenter] are in the same state of mind, and that is not the same state of mind as you or he are in when asleep. He is inviting you and himself to be prejudiced in favour of a state of mind in which we are when awake.
>
> (p. 142)

In other words, what the patient is calling *dreams*, we would call *hallucinations*. The patient cannot differentiate visual events that he has while sleeping from visual perceptions he has when he is "awake." He is "inviting you and himself to be prejudiced in favour of a state of mind in which we are when awake," i.e. he is trying to convince the analyst that there is only one state – that of being awake – so that both patient and analyst can agree that the patient is not psychotic and is simply reporting what he perceives in a waking state. The patient is insisting that because there is only one state – that of wakefulness – there is no difference between perception and hallucination, dream-life and waking-life; consequently, there is no such thing as psychosis.

The element of Bion's analytic style with which I am concerned here is the absolute directness with which he speaks to the (dreamt-up) patient. He senses almost immediately when the patient is using words in a way that involves a slippage of meaning that prevents painful recognition of the truth. Bion, as in the instance under discussion, then speaks to the patient in a way that restores the proper meaning to words, which in turn allows for thinking and "ordinary human intercourse" (p. 197) to begin or resume. To be able consistently to hear and respond to such slippages of meaning requires a very fine ear indeed.

Concluding comments

It is impossible to give an adequate rendering of an analyst's style since his style is informed by nothing less than everything that he is as a person and as an analyst. Though I greatly admire many of the qualities of Bion's analytic style that are brought to life in the "Clinical seminars," I do not view his style as a model to emulate. Rather, as Bion states in the seminars, "The way I do psychoanalysis is of no importance to anybody excepting myself, but it may give you some idea of how *you* do analysis, and that *is* important" (p. 224).

8

Reading Loewald

Oedipus reconceived

In the history of psychoanalysis, Freud's Oedipus complex has been reinvented several times – for example, by Klein, Fairbairn, Lacan and Kohut. At the heart of Loewald's (1979) re-conceptualization of the Oedipus complex is the idea that it is the task of each new generation to make use of, destroy and reinvent the creations of the previous generation. Loewald reformulates the Oedipus complex in a way that provides fresh ways of viewing many of the fundamental human tasks entailed in growing up, growing old and, in between the two, managing to make something of one's own that succeeding generations might make use of to create something unique of their own. Thus, Loewald reinvents Freud's version of the Oedipus complex, and it is my task to reconceive Loewald's version of the Oedipus complex in the very act of presenting it. By means of a close reading of Loewald's (1979) "The waning of the Oedipus complex," I will demonstrate what it is about the way Loewald thinks that leads me to view that paper as a watershed in the development of psycho-analytic thought.

The sequential nature of writing makes it difficult for Loewald to capture the simultaneity of the elements of the Oedipus complex; I, too, must struggle with this dilemma. I have elected to discuss Loewald's overlapping ideas in more or less the sequence he presents them, addressing the tension between influence and originality in the succession of generations; the murder of the oedipal parents and the appropriation of their authority; the metamorphic internalization of the child's experience of the parents which underlies the formation of a self responsible for itself and to itself; and the transitional incestuous

138 *Change in forme*
(though text & pressure)

object relationship which mediates the dialectical interplay between differentiated and undifferentiated forms of object relatedness. I conclude with a comparison of Freud's and Loewald's conceptions of the Oedipus complex.

Freud's theory of the Oedipus complex

In order to place Loewald's contribution in context, I will review the major tenets of Freud's Oedipus complex, as I understand them. Freud's conception of the Oedipus complex is built on a foundation of four revolutionary ideas: (1) All of human psychology and psycho-pathology, as well as all human cultural achievements, can be under-stood in terms of urges and meanings that have their roots in the sexual and aggressive instincts; (2) The sexual instinct is experienced as a driving force beginning at birth and is elaborated sequentially in its oral, anal and phallic components in the course of the first five years of life; (3) Of the multitude of myths and stories that human beings have created, the myth of Oedipus, for psychoanalysis, is the single most important narrative organizing human psychological development; and (4) The triangulated set of conflictual murderous and incestuous fantasies constituting the Oedipus complex is "deter-mined and laid down by heredity" (Freud, 1924, p. 174) – that is, it is a manifestation of a universal, inborn propensity of human beings to organize experience in this particular way (see Ogden, 1986).

The Oedipus complex for Freud (1924) is "contemporaneous" (p. 174) with the phallic phase of sexual development. It is a web of intrapsychic and interpersonal parent–child relationships in which the boy, for example, takes his mother as the object of his romantic and sexual desire, and wishes to take his father's place with his mother (Freud, 1910, 1921, 1923, 1924, 1925). The father is simultaneously admired and viewed as a punitive rival. The aggressive instinct is manifested, for the boy, in the form of the wish to kill his father in order to have his mother for himself. The wish to kill the father is a highly ambivalent one, given the boy's pre-oedipal love for and identification with his father, as well as the boy's erotic attachment to his father in the negative Oedipus complex (Freud, 1921). The boy experiences guilt in response to his wish to murder his father (in the positive Oedipus complex) and his mother (in the negative Oedipus complex). Similarly, the girl takes her father as the object of her desire, and wishes to take her mother's place with her father. She, too, experiences guilt in response to her incestuous and murderous wishes in the complete Oedipus complex (Freud, 1921, 1925).

The child guiltily fears punishment for his or her murderous and incestuous wishes in the form of castration at the hands of the father. Whether or not actual castration threats are made, the threat of castration is present in the mind of the child as a "primal phantasy" (Freud, 1916–17, p. 370), a universal unconscious fantasy that is part of the make-up of the human psyche.

"Analytic observation[s] . . . justify the statement that the destruction of the Oedipus complex is brought about by the threat of castration" (Freud, 1924, p. 177). That is, the child, for fear of punishment in the form of castration, relinquishes his or her sexual and aggressive strivings in relation to the oedipal parents and replaces those "object cathexes . . . [with] identifications" (ibid., p. 176) with parental authority, prohibitions and ideals, which form the core of a new psychic structure, the superego.

The tension between influence and originality

With Freud's conception of the Oedipus complex in mind, I will now turn to Loewald's reformulation. The opening sentence of Loewald's paper is a curious one in that it appears to make no reference to the subject that the paper will address: "Many of the views expressed in this paper have been stated previously by others" (p. 384) (all page references not otherwise specified refer to Loewald's [1979] "The waning of the Oedipus complex"). Why would anyone begin a psychoanalytic paper with a disclaimer renouncing claims for originality? Loewald goes on immediately (still not giving the reader a rationale for his odd approach) to cite a lengthy passage from Breuer's introduction to the theoretical section of *Studies on Hysteria*:

> When a science is making rapid advances, thoughts which were first expressed by single individuals quickly become common property. Thus no one who attempts to put forward today his views on hysteria and its psychical basis can avoid repeating a great quantity of other people's thoughts, which are in the act of passing from personal into general possession. It is scarcely possible always to be certain who first gave them utterance, and there is always a

danger of regarding as a product of one's own what has already been said by someone else. I hope, therefore, that I may be excused if few quotations are found in this discussion and if no strict distinction is made between what is my own and what originates elsewhere. Originality is claimed for very little of what will be found in the following pages (Breuer and Freud, 1893–1895, pp. 185–186; cited in Loewald, 1979, p. 384).

Subliminally, a sense of cyclical time is created by the juxtaposition of Loewald's disclaiming originality and Breuer's virtually identical statement made almost a century earlier. Loewald, before discussing his ideas concerning the Oedipus complex, is showing them to us in our experience of reading: no generation has the right to claim absolute originality for its creations (see Ogden, 2003b, 2005b). And yet, each new generation does contribute something uniquely its own: "Many [not all] of the views expressed in this paper have been stated previously" (Loewald); and "Originality is claimed for very little [but something]" (Breuer).[1]

Between the lines of Loewald's text is the idea that it is the fate of the child (as it was the fate of the parents) that what he makes of his own will enter a process of "passing from personal into general possession" (Breuer). In other words, what we do manage to create that bears our own mark will become part of the pool of collective knowledge and, in so doing, we become nameless, but not insignificant ancestors to succeeding generations: "there is always a danger of regarding as a product of one's own what has already been said by someone else" (Breuer), an ancestor whose name has been lost to us.

Loewald's paper goes on to both explore and bring to life this tension between one's indebtedness to one's forbears and one's wish to free oneself from them in the process of becoming a person on one's own terms. This tension between influence and originality lies at the core of the Oedipus complex, as Loewald conceives of it.

---

1 Breuer's words echo those written by Plato two-and-a-half millennia earlier: "Now I am well aware that none of these ideas can have come from me – I know my own ignorance. The only other possibility, I think, is that I was filled, like an empty jar, by the words of other people streaming in through my ears, though I'm so stupid that I've even forgotten where and from whom I heard them" (*Phaedrus*, 1997, p. 514). Loewald, trained in philosophy, no doubt was familiar with this dialogue.

More than a repression

The paper seems to begin again in its second paragraph with a definition of the Oedipus complex as the "psychic representation of a central, instinctually motivated, triangular conflictual constellation of child–parent relations" (p. 384). (With its several beginnings and several endings, the paper itself embodies the multiplicity of births and deaths that mark the endless cycle of generations.) Loewald then draws our attention to the way in which Freud (1923, 1925), in speaking of the fate of the Oedipus complex, uses forceful language, referring to its "destruction" (Freud, 1924, p. 177) and its "demolition" (Freud, 1925, p. 257). Moreover, Freud (1924) insists, "If the ego has . . . not achieved much more than a repression of the complex, the latter persists in an unconscious state . . . and will later manifest its pathogenic effect" (p. 177). This idea provides Loewald the key to his understanding of the fate of the Oedipus complex.

The reader's head begins to swim at this point as a consequence of the convergence of two interrelated enigmatic ideas: (1) the notion that the Oedipus complex is "demolished" (how are we to understand the idea that some of the most important human experiences are, in health, destroyed?); and (2) the idea that the demolition of the Oedipus complex is "more than a repression" (whatever that means). The reader, here and throughout the paper, must do a good deal of thinking for himself in making something of his own with the ideas that Loewald is presenting. This, after all, is the task of each new generation vis-à-vis the creations of its ancestors.

In an effort to find his bearings in this portion of the paper, the reader must grapple with several questions. To begin with, the reader must determine the meaning of the term *repression* as it is being used here. Freud uses the term to refer to two overlapping but distinct ideas in the course of his writing. At times, he uses the term to refer to psychological operations that serve to establish "the unconscious as a domain separate from the rest of the psyche" (Laplanche and Pontalis, 1967, p. 390), a *sine qua non* of psychological health. At other times – including, I believe, the instance under discussion – the term is used to refer to a pathogenic expulsion from consciousness of disturbing thoughts and feelings. Not only is the repressed segregated from the main body of conscious thought, but repressed thoughts and feelings are, for the most part, cut off from conscious and unconscious psychological work.

The reader must also attempt to formulate for himself what it means to bring the Oedipus complex to a close not by repressing it, but by demolishing the thoughts, feelings, bodily sensations and object-related experiences that constitute it. To my mind – and I think that there would be general agreement among psychoanalysts on this point – the psychic registration of a significant experience, whether that registration be conscious or unconscious, is never destroyed. It may be suppressed, repressed, displaced, denied, disowned, dissociated, projected, introjected, split off, foreclosed and so on, but never destroyed or demolished. No experience can ever "unhappen" psychically. And yet this is what Freud and Loewald are insisting to be the case – at least to a significant degree – in the waning of the Oedipus complex. The unresolved question of what it means to say that the Oedipus complex undergoes "more than a repression" (i.e. that it is demolished) generates in the experience of reading Loewald's paper a tension that is not unlike the experience of living with unresolved (but not repressed) oedipal conflict. It unsettles everything it touches in a vitalizing way.

Parricide: A loving murder

Having introduced these thoughts and questions regarding the demolition of the Oedipus complex, Loewald proceeds to broaden the traditional conception of the oedipal murder. He uses the term parricide to refer to the act committed by "One who murders a person to whom he stands in a specially sacred relation, as a father, mother, or other near relative, or (in a wider sense) a ruler. Sometimes, one guilty of treason (*Webster, International Dictionary, 2nd ed.*)" (cited in Loewald, 1979, p. 387).[2] In the act of parricide, Loewald observes,

> It is a parental authority that is murdered; by that, whatever is sacred about the bond between child and parent is violated. If we take etymology as a guide, it is bringing forth, nourishing,

---

2 Loewald uses the word *sacred* as a secular term to refer to that which is solemnly, respect-fully set apart, as poetry, for Plato and Borges, is set apart from other forms of human expressiveness – poetry is "something winged, light and sacred" (Plato, cited in Borges, 1984, p. 32).

providing for, and protecting of the child by the parents that constitute their parenthood, authority (authorship), and render sacred the child's ties with the parents. Parricide is a crime against the sanctity of such a bond.

(p. 387)

Loewald again and again in his paper makes use of etymology – the ancestry of words, the history of the way succeeding generations both draw upon and alter the meanings of words.

Parricide involves a revolt against parental authority and parental claims to authorship of the child. That revolt involves not a ceremonious passing of the baton from one generation to the next, but a murder in which a sacred bond is severed. The child's breaking of the sacred bond to the parents does not represent a fearful response to the threat of bodily mutilation (castration), but a passionate assertion of the "active urge for emancipation" (p. 389) from the parents. Loewald's phrase *urge for emancipation* connects the word *urge* (which has a strong tie to the bodily instinctual drives) with the word *emancipation*, thus generating the idea of an innate drive for individuation. In the language itself, instinct theory is being broadened by Loewald to include drives beyond the sexual and aggressive urges (see Chodorow, 2003; Kaywin, 1993; and Mitchell, 1998, for discussions of the relationship between instinct theory and object relations theory in Loewald's work).

In the oedipal battle, "opponents are required" (p. 389). A relative absence of genuine parental authority leaves the child with little to appropriate. Moreover, when the parents' authority has not been established, the child's fantasies lack "brakes" (Winnicott, 1945, p. 153) – that is, the secure knowledge that his fantasies will not be allowed to be played out in reality. When parental authority does not provide the "brakes" for fantasy, the fantasied murder of those one loves and depends upon is too frightening to endure. Under such pathological circumstances, the child, in an effort to defend himself against the danger of the actual murder of the parents, represses (buries alive) his murderous impulses and enforces that repression by adopting a harshly punitive stance toward these feelings. In health, paradoxically, the felt presence of parental authority makes it possible for the child to safely murder his parents psychically (a fantasy that need not be repressed). Oedipal parricide does not require repression because it is ultimately a loving act, a "passionate appropriation of what is experienced as loveable and admirable in parents" (p. 396). In

144

a sense, the fantasied death of one's oedipal parents is "collateral damage" in the child's struggle for independence and individuation. Killing one's parents is not an end in itself.

For Loewald, the Oedipus complex is at its core a face-off between the generations, a life-and-death battle for autonomy, authority and responsibility. In this struggle, parents are "actively rejected, fought against, and destroyed, to varying degrees" (pp. 388–389). Difficulty arises not from parricidal fantasies per se, but from an inability to safely commit parricide, to sever one's oedipal ties to one's parents. The following brief clinical account illustrates a form of difficulty encountered in the oedipal appropriation of parental authority:

Several years into his analysis, Mr. N told me the following dream: "I was checking in at the front desk of a hotel late at night. The man behind the desk told me that all the rooms were booked. I said that I had heard that hotels keep a few rooms open in case someone shows up in the middle of the night. I thought, but did not say to him, that those rooms are meant for important people. I knew that I was not an important person. At the other end of the long desk, an older woman who was checking in said in a commanding voice, 'He's with me – he'll share my room.' I didn't want to share a room with her. The thought was repellent. I felt as if I couldn't get a breath of air and tried to find a way out of the hotel, but I couldn't find an exit."

Mr. N said that he felt extremely embarrassed by the dream and had considered not mentioning it to me. He told me that even though we had often talked about his feeling that his parents had had no psychological room in themselves for him as a child, he was horrified in the dream by the woman (who seemed like his mother) offering to have him share her room, and, by implication, her bed, with him.

I said to Mr. N that the embarrassment he felt in response to the dream may stem not only from his feeling horrified by the idea of sleeping with his mother, but also from seeing himself as a perennial child who lacks the authority to claim a place of his own among adults – a boy who will never become a man.

By contrast, an experience in the analysis of a man in his mid-twenties captures something of the experience of a healthy oedipal succession of generations:

A medical student near the end of his analysis with me began affectionately to refer to me as "a geezer" after it had become apparent that I knew very little of the developments in psychopharmacology that had occurred in the previous 25 years. I was reminded of my own first analysis, which had begun while I was a medical student. My analyst occasionally referred to himself as an "old buck" in response to my competitiveness with him regarding what I was learning about current developments in psychoanalysis. I remembered having been surprised by his seemingly calm acceptance of his place in the "over-the-hill" generation of analysts and of my place in the new (and, I believed, far more dynamic) generation.

While with my medical student analysand, my memory of my analyst's referring to himself as an old buck struck me as both comic and disturbing – disturbing in that at the time he said it, he was younger than I was at that juncture in the analysis of my patient. I recognized how his acceptance of his place in the succession of generations was currently of great value to me in my efforts not only to accept, but also, in a certain way, to embrace my place as "a geezer" in the analysis of my medical student.

As parents to our children, even as we fight to maintain our parental authority, we allow ourselves to be killed by our children lest we "diminish them" (p. 395). In the Oedipus myth, Laius and Jocasta are told by the oracle at Delphi that their son is destined to murder his father. The horror of this prophecy is equivalent in present-day terms to a hospital forewarning each couple as they enter the obstetrics ward that their child who is about to be born will one day murder them. Laius and Jocasta attempt to circumvent such an outcome by killing their child. But they cannot bring themselves to commit the murder by their own hand. They give Oedipus to a shepherd who is told to leave the infant in the forest to die. In so doing, Laius and Jocasta unconsciously collude in their own murder. They create a window of opportunity for their child not only to survive, but also to grow up to murder them.[3]

The dilemma faced by Laius and Jocasta is a dilemma shared not only by all parents, but also by all analysts when we begin analysis

---

3 The Oedipus complex is, in a sense, a process by which the child, in killing his parents (with their cooperation), creates his own ancestors (see Borges, 1962).

with a new patient. In beginning analysis, we as analysts are setting in motion a process in which the patient – if all goes well – will contribute to our dying. For all to go well, we must allow ourselves to be killed by our patients lest "we diminish them" (p. 395), for example, by treating them as less mature than they are, by giving advice that is not needed, supportive tones of voice that are unwanted, and interpretations that are undermining of the patient's ability to think reflectively and insightfully for himself. Not to diminish one's children (and one's patients) involves not a passive resignation to aging and death, but an actively loving gesture repeated time and again in which one gives over one's place in the present generation to take one's place sadly and proudly among those in the process of becoming ancestors. Resistance to taking one's place as part of the past generation will not stop the succession of generations, but it will leave a felt absence in the lives of one's children and grandchildren, an absence where their ancestors might under other circumstances have been a highly valued presence. (Loewald told his colleague, Bryce Boyer, that he could not have written this paper before he became a grandfather [Boyer, 1999, personal communication].)

Parents may try to protect themselves against giving way to the next generation by behaving as if there is no difference between the generations. For example, when parents do not close bedroom and bathroom doors, or display erotic photographs as "art," or do not wear clothing at home because "the human body is not a shameful thing," they are implicitly claiming that there is no generational difference – children and adults are equal. Children, under such circumstances, have no genuine parental objects to kill and only a perverse version of parental authority to appropriate. This leaves the individual a stunted child frozen in time.

Having discussed the central role in the Oedipus complex of the child's loving murder of his parents, Loewald makes a remarkable statement that sets this paper apart from its psychoanalytic predecessors:

> If we do not shrink from blunt language, in our role as children of our parents, by genuine emancipation we do kill something vital in them – not all in one blow and not in all respects, but contributing to their dying.

> (p. 395)

147

In the space of a single sentence, the Oedipus complex is radically reconceived. It had been well established by Freud (1909, 1910) that the Oedipus complex is not simply an intrapsychic event, but a set of living object relationships between the child and his parents. But Loewald does not stop there. For him, the fantasied murder of the parents that is played out in oedipal object relationships contributes to – is part of the process of – the parents' dying. It is tempting to water down Loewald's "blunt language" by saying that "their dying" is a metaphor for parents' relinquishing their authority over (their authorship of) the life of the child. But Loewald is saying more than that: he is insisting that the living out of the Oedipus complex by children and their parents is part of the emotional process (which is inseparable from bodily processes) by which human beings grow up, grow old, and die.

The battle between parents and children for autonomy and authority is most evident in adolescence and beyond, but it is, of course, equally important in early childhood. This is true not only of the child's falling in love with one parent while becoming intensely jealous of, and rivalrous with, the other. In addition, for example, the "terrible twos" often involves the parents in a battle with their newly ambulatory child who is relentlessly insistent on his independence. Parents of two-year-olds frequently experience their child's "stubborn willfulness" as a betrayal of an unspoken agreement that the child will remain a fully dependent, adored and adoring baby "forever." The child's breaking of the "agreement" constitutes an assault on the parents' wish to remain parents of a baby timelessly, i.e. insulated from the passage of time, aging, death and the succession of generations. (The relationship of the "stubborn" toddler to his parents is triangulated to the degree that the child splits the parents intrapsychically into the good and the bad parent or parents.)

The metamorphic internalization of the oedipal parents

Thus, parricide, from the point of view of both parents and children, is a necessary path to the child's growing up, his coming to life as an adult who has attained authority in his own right. Oedipal parricide conceived of in this way underlies, for both Freud and Loewald, the organization of "the superego [which is] the culmination of individual psychic structure formation" (Loewald, 1979, p. 404). The use of the term *superego* in this phrase and throughout Loewald's paper represents a residue of the structural model of the mind that Loewald is in the process of transforming. Consequently, the term, as used by Loewald, is confusing. As I read his paper, I find it clarifying to my thinking to "translate" the term *superego* into terms that are more in keeping with the ideas that Loewald is developing. In place of the word *superego*, I use the idea of an aspect of the self (derived from appropriated parental authority) that takes the measure of and the responsibility for who one is and how one conducts oneself.

Superego formation involves an "internalization" (Loewald, p. 390) of or "identification" (Loewald, p. 391) with the oedipal parents. (Freud [1921, 1923, 1924, 1925], too, repeatedly uses the terms *identification, introjection*, and *incorporation* to describe the process of superego formation.) This brings us to what I consider to be one of the most difficult and most important questions raised by Loewald regarding the Oedipus complex: what does it mean to say that oedipal object relationships are internalized in the process of superego organization? Loewald responds to this question in a very dense passage that leaves a great deal unsaid or merely suggested. I will offer a close reading of this passage in which I include inferences that I have drawn from Loewald's statements:

> The organization of the superego, as internalization . . . of oedipal object relations, documents parricide and at the same time is its atonement and metamorphosis: atonement insofar as the superego makes up for and is a restitution of oedipal relationships; metamorphosis insofar as in this restitution oedipal object relations are transmuted into internal, intrapsychic structural relations.
>
> (p. 389)

To paraphrase the opening portion of this passage, the organization of the superego "documents" parricide in the sense that superego organization is living proof of the murder of the parents. The superego embodies the child's successful appropriation of parental authority which is transformed into the child's capacities for autonomy and responsibility. The superego as psychic structure monitors the ego and, in this sense, takes responsibility for the ego/*das Ich*/the I.

That same process of superego organization constitutes not only an internal record of parricide in the form of an alteration of the psyche of the child, but also an "atonement" (p. 389) for the murder of the

149

parents. As I understand it, the organization of the superego represents an atonement for parricide in that, at the same moment that the child murders the parents (psychically), he bestows upon them a form of immortality. That is, by incorporating the child's experience of his parents (albeit, a "transmuted" version of them) into the very structure of who he is as an individual, the child secures the parents a place, a seat of influence, not only in the way the child conducts his life, but also in the way the child's children conduct their lives, and on and on. I am using the word *children* here both literally and metaphorically. The alteration of the psyche involved in superego organization influences not simply the way the grown child relates to his own children; it affects everything that the child creates in the course of his life, for example, the qualities of the friendships and other love relationships in which he takes part, as well as the thinking and creativity that he brings to the work that he does. These creations (his literal and metaphorical children) alter those they touch, who in turn, alter those they touch.

The "internalization" of the parents (in a transformed state) constitutes atonement for killing the parents in that this internalization contributes to the child's becoming like the parents. But, in another sense, it is in the "transmutation" of the parents that an even more profound form of atonement lies. To the extent that the parents have been transformed in the internalization process, the parents have contributed to the creation of a child who is capable of being and becoming *unlike them* – that is, capable of becoming a person who is, in certain respects, more than the people who the parents have been capable of being and becoming. What more meaningful atonement can there be for killing one's parents?

Loewald continues in the passage under discussion: superego organization is an atonement for parricide "insofar as the superego makes up for and is a restitution of oedipal object relations." These words are carefully chosen. The word *restitution* derives from the Latin word meaning *to re-establish*. The formation of the superego restores to the parents their authority as parents – but not the same authority that they formerly held as parents. Now they are parents to a child who is increasingly capable of being responsible for himself and to himself as an autonomous person. The parents who are "restituted" (re-established) are parents who had not previously existed (or, perhaps more accurately, had existed only as a potential).

For Loewald, in the passage under discussion, superego formation as a part of the resolution of the Oedipus complex represents not only an atonement for parricide and the restitution of the parents, but also a "metamorphosis insofar as in this restitution oedipal object relations are transmuted into internal, intrapsychic structural relations" (p. 389). I find the metaphor of metamorphosis to be critical to Loewald's conception of what it means to say that the parents are internalized in a "transmuted" form. (Loewald, in this paper, uses the word *metamorphosis* only in the sentence being cited and may not have been aware of the full implications of his use of this metaphor.) In complete metamorphosis, for example, in the life cycle of the butterfly, inside the cocoon, the tissues of the caterpillar (the larva) break down. A few clusters of cells from the breakdown of the larval tissues constitute the beginning of a new cellular organization from which adult structures are generated (e.g. wings, eyes, tongue, antennae and body segments).

There is continuity (the DNA of the caterpillar and that of the butterfly are identical) and discontinuity (there is a vast difference between the morphology and physiology of the external and internal structures of the caterpillar and that of the butterfly). So, too, superego formation (the internalization of oedipal object relations) involves a simultaneity of continuity and radical transformation. The parents (as experienced by the child) are not internalized, any more than a caterpillar sprouts wings. The child's "internalization" of oedipal object relationships involves a profound transformation of his experience of his parents (analogous to the breakdown of the bodily structure of the caterpillar) before they are restituted in the form of the organization of the child's more mature psychic structure (superego formation).[4]

In other words, the child's "internalized" oedipal object relationships (constituting the superego) have their origins in the "DNA" of the parents – that is, the unconscious psychological make-up of the parents (which in turn "documents" their own oedipal object relationships

---

4 A passage from Karp and Berrill's (1981) classic, *Development*, underscores the aptness of the metaphor of metamorphosis: "The completion of the cocoon signals the beginning of a new and even more remarkable sequence of events. On the third day after a cocoon is finished, a great wave of death and destruction sweeps over the internal organs of the caterpillar. The specialized larval tissues break down, but meanwhile, certain more or less discrete clusters of cells, tucked away here and there in the body, begin to grow rapidly, nourishing themselves on the breakdown products of the dead and dying larval tissues. These are the imaginal discs . . . Their spurt of growth now shapes the organism according to a new plan. New organs arise from the discs" (p. 692).

with their parents). At the same time, despite this powerful transgenerational continuity of oedipal experience, if the child (with the parents' help) is able to kill his oedipal parents, he creates a psychological clearance in which to enter into libidinal relationships with "novel" (p. 390) (non-incestuous) objects. These novel relationships have a life of their own outside of the terms of the child's libidinal and aggressive relationships with his oedipal parents. In this way, genuinely novel (non-incestuous) relationships with one's parents and others become possible. (The novel object relationships are colored, but not dominated, by transferences to the oedipal parents.)

In a single summary sentence, which could have been written by no one other than Loewald, the elements of the transformations involved in superego formation (the establishment of an autonomous, responsible self) are brought together: "The self, in its autonomy, is an atonement structure, a structure of reconciliation, and as such a supreme achievement" (p. 394).

The transitional incestuous object relationship

The paper begins anew as Loewald takes up the incestuous component of the Oedipus complex. This portion of the paper, for me, lacks the power of the foregoing discussion of imagined (and real) parricide, guilt, atonement, and restitution. It seems to me that the centerpiece of the paper – and Loewald's principal interest – is the role of the Oedipus complex in the child's achievement of an autonomous, responsible self. Incestuous desire is a subsidiary theme in that story.

Loewald opens his discussion of oedipal incestuous wishes by raising the rarely asked (even a bit startling) question: What's wrong with incest? He responds, "Incestuous object relations are evil, according to received morality, in that they interfere with or destroy that sacred bond . . . the original oneness, most obvious in the mother–infant dual unity" (p. 396). Incest involves the intrusion of differentiated libidinal object relatedness into the " 'sacred' innocence of primary narcissistic unity . . . [which is] anterior to individuation and its inherent guilt and atonement" (p. 396).

In other words, we view incest as evil because, in incest, differentiated, object-related sexual desire is directed toward the very same person (and the very same body) with whom an undifferentiated bond (which we hold sacred) existed and continues to exist. Thus, for Loewald, incest is felt to be wrong, not primarily because it represents a challenge to the father's authority and a claim to the mother, or because it denies the difference between the generations, but because it destroys the demarcation between a fused form of mother–child relatedness (primary identification) and a differentiated object relatedness with the same person. Incest is felt to be evil because it overturns the "barrier between [primary] identification [at-one-ment] and [differentiated] object cathexis" (p. 397).

The overturning of the barrier between primary identification and object cathexis is a matter of the greatest importance, not only because the individual's emerging sexuality is shaped by the way the parents and children handle incestuous desire, but, perhaps even more importantly, because the individual's capacity for healthy object relatedness of every sort – his capacity to establish a generative dialectic of separateness from, and union with, other people – depends upon the living integrity of that barrier.

Parricide is a manifestation of the oedipal child's drive to become an autonomous individual; incestuous wishes and fantasies represent the concurrent need on the part of the oedipal child for unity with the mother. From this vantage point, "The incestuous [oedipal] object thus is an intermediate, ambiguous entity, neither a full-fledged libidinal objectum [differentiated object] nor an unequivocal identificatum [undifferentiated object]" (p. 397). Loewald uses the terms *incestuous object* and *incestuous object relationship* to refer not to actual incest, but to external and internal object relationships in which incestuous fantasies predominate. The incestuous oedipal relationship persists as an ongoing aspect of the Oedipus complex, which mediates the tension between the urge for autonomy and responsibility and the healthy pull toward unity (for example, as an aspect of falling in love, empathy, sexuality, caregiving, "primary maternal preoccupation" [Winnicott, 1956, p. 300], and so on).

Both the superego and the transitional incestuous object relationship are heirs to the Oedipus complex in complementary ways, each mediating a tension between love of the parents and the wish to emancipate oneself from them and to establish novel object relationships. There are, however, important differences between the two. The atonement (at-one-ment) that underlies superego formation involves the metamorphic internalization of an object relationship with the parents as whole and separate objects; by contrast, the at-one-ment involved in (transitional) incestuous object relatedness is that of fusion with the parents (primary identification).

By understanding the oedipal incestuous object relationship as constituting an intermediate position between undifferentiated and differentiated object relatedness, Loewald is not simply amplifying a psychoanalytic conception of pre-oedipal development. He is suggesting something more. The Oedipus complex is not only a set of differentiated object relationships that comprise "the neurotic core" (p. 400) of the personality. The Oedipus complex "contains . . . in its very core" (p. 399) a more archaic set of object relationships that constitutes the "psychotic core" (p. 400) of the personality. From the latter, the earliest forms of healthy separation-individuation emerge.

Thus, the Oedipus complex is the emotional crucible in which the entirety of the personality is forged as the oedipal configuration is reworked and reorganized on increasingly more mature planes throughout the individual's life (see Ogden, 1987). Loewald, not one to claim originality for his ideas, states that while Freud "acknowledged the fact [that the Oedipus complex centrally involves undifferentiated object relations] long ago" (Loewald, 1979, p. 399), this aspect of the Oedipus complex is "more [important] than was realized by Freud" (p. 399). This more primitive aspect of the Oedipus complex is not outgrown; rather, it takes its place as "a deep layer of advanced mentality" (p. 402).

Before concluding this part of the discussion, I will revisit an idea that remains unresolved. At the outset of the paper, Loewald (with Freud) insisted that in health the Oedipus complex is "demolished." Loewald, in the course of the paper, modifies that idea:

> In the abstract, as the organization of this structure [the autonomous self] proceeds, the Oedipus complex would be destroyed as a constellation of object relations or their fantasy representations. But, in the words of Ariel in Shakespeare's *Tempest*, nothing fades, "but doth suffer a sea-change into something rich and strange."
>
> (p. 394)

In other words, the Oedipus complex is not destroyed, but is continually in the process of being transformed into "something rich and strange," that is, into a multitude of evolving, forever problematic aspects of the human condition which constitute "the troubling but rewarding richness of life" (p. 400). The reader may wonder why Loewald does not say so from the beginning instead of invoking the clearly untenable idea that experience can be destroyed. I believe that Loewald begins with more absolute and dramatic language because there is a truth to it that he does not want the reader to lose sight of: to the degree that one succeeds in murdering one's parents psychically and atones for that parricide in a way that contributes to the formation of an autonomous self, one is released from the emotional confines of the Oedipus complex. The Oedipus complex is destroyed to the extent that oedipal relationships with one's parents no longer constitute the conscious and unconscious emotional world within which the individual lives as a perennial, dependent child.

The paper closes as it began, with a comment addressing writing itself as opposed to the subject matter that has been taken up:

> I am aware that, perhaps confusingly, I have shifted perspectives several times in my presentation. I hope that the composite picture I have tried to sketch in this fashion has not become too blurred by my approach.

> (p. 404)

The words, *shift[ing] perspectives*, to my ear, describe a style of writing and thinking that is always in the process of being revised, and a style of reading that is as critically questioning as it is receptive to the ideas being presented. What more suitable ending can one imagine for a paper that addresses the ways in which one generation leaves its mark on the next, and yet fosters in its descendants the exercise of their right and responsibility to become authors of their own ideas and ways of conducting themselves?

Loewald and Freud

I will conclude by highlighting some of the differences between Loewald's and Freud's conceptions of the Oedipus complex. For Loewald, the Oedipus complex is driven not primarily by the child's sexual and aggressive impulses (as it is for Freud), but by the "urge for emancipation," the need to become an autonomous individual. The girl, for example, is not most fundamentally driven to take the place of her mother in the parents' bed, but to take her parents' authority as

155

her own. The child atones for imagined (and real) parricide by means of a metamorphic internalization of the oedipal parents which results in an alteration of the self (the formation of a new psychic agency, the superego). "Responsibility to oneself . . . is the essence of superego as internal agency" (Loewald, 1979, p. 392). Thus, the child repays the parents in the most meaningful terms possible – that is, by establishing a sense of self that is responsible to oneself and for oneself, a self that may be capable of becoming a person who is, in ways, more than the people who the parents were capable of being and becoming.

The incestuous component of the Oedipus complex contributes to the maturation of the self by serving as an ambiguous, transitional form of object relatedness that holds in tension with one another differentiated and undifferentiated dimensions of mature object ties. The Oedipus complex is brought to an end not by a fear-driven response to the threat of castration, but by the child's need to atone for parricide and to restore to the parents their (now transformed) authority as parents.

I do not view Loewald's version of the Oedipus complex as an updated version of Freud's. Rather, to my mind, the two renderings of the Oedipus complex constitute different perspectives from which to view the same phenomena. Both perspectives are indispensable to a contemporary psychoanalytic understanding of the Oedipus complex.

9

Harold Searles' "Oedipal love in the countertransference" and "Unconscious identification"

No other analytic writer, to my mind, rivals Searles in his ability to capture in words his observations concerning his emotional response to what is occurring in the analytic relationship and his use of these observations in his effort to understand and interpret the transference–countertransference. I offer here close readings of portions of two of Searles' papers, "Oedipal love in the countertrans-ference" (1959) and "Unconscious identification" (1990), in which I describe not only *what* Searles thinks, but what I believe to be the essence of *the way* Searles thinks and *how* he works in the analytic setting. Being receptive to what is occurring at a given moment in an analysis involves, for Searles, an exquisite sensitivity to the uncon-scious communications of the patient. Such receptivity to the patient's unconscious communications requires of the analyst a form of laying bare his own unconscious experience. Searles' way of using himself analytically very often entails a blurring of the distinction between his own conscious and unconscious experience as well as the distinc-tion between his unconscious experience and that of the patient. As a result, Searles' comments to the patient (and to the reader) concerning what he understands to be occurring between himself and the patient are often startling to the reader, but almost always utilizable by the patient (and the reader) for purposes of conscious and unconscious psychological work.

In discussing "Oedipal love in the countertransference," I focus on the way in which, for Searles, unflinchingly accurate clinical observation spawns original clinical theory (in this instance, a reconceptualization of the Oedipus complex). When I speak of *clinical theory*, I am referring to proposed experience-near understandings (formulated in terms of thoughts, feelings and behaviour) of phenomena occurring in the clinical setting. Transference, for example, is a clinical theory that proposes that certain of the patient's feelings towards the analyst, unbeknownst to the patient, have their origins in feelings that the patient experienced in previous real and imagined object relationships, usually childhood relationships. By contrast, psychoanalytic theories involving higher levels of abstraction (for example, Freud's topographic model, Klein's concept of the internal object world, and Bion's theory of alpha function) propose spatial and other types of metaphor as ways of thinking about how the mind works.

In my reading of "Unconscious identification," I suggest that Searles has a distinctive way of thinking and working analytically which might be thought of as a process of "turning experience inside out." By this I mean that Searles transforms what had been an invisible and yet felt presence, an emotional context, into psychological content about which the patient may be able to think and speak. What had been a frightening, unnamed, fully taken for granted quality of the patient's internal and external world is transformed by Searles into a verbally symbolized emotional dilemma about which the analytic pair may be able to think and converse.

Finally, I discuss what I view as the complementarity between Searles' work and that of Bion. I have found that reading Searles provides a vibrant clinical context for Bion's work, and reading Bion provides a valuable theoretical context for Searles' work. I focus, in particular, on the mutually enriching "conversation" (created in the mind of the reader) between Searles' clinical work and Bion's concepts of the container–contained, the fundamental human need for truth and Bion's reconceptualization of the relationship between conscious and unconscious experience.

Oedipal love in the countertransference

In the opening pages of the "Oedipal love" paper, Searles provides a thoughtful review of the analytic literature concerning countertransference love. The consensus on this topic current at the time was succinctly articulated by Tower (1956, cited in Searles, 1959, p. 285):

"Virtually every writer on the subject of countertransference . . . states unequivocally that no form of erotic reaction to a patient is to be tolerated . . ." With this sentiment looming in the background, Searles presents an analytic experience that occurred in the latter part of a four-year analysis (which he conducted early in his career). He tells us that the patient's femininity had initially been "considerably repressed" (1959, p. 290). In the last year of this analysis, Searles found himself having "abundant desires to be married to her, and fantasies of being her husband" (1959, p. 290). Blunt acknowledgement of such thoughts and feelings was unprecedented in 1959, and, even today, is a rare occurrence in the analytic literature. The word *marry* – such an ordinary word – is strangely powerful as a consequence of its connotations both of falling in love and of wishes to make a family and to live everyday life with the person one loves. It seems to me highly significant that the fantasies described by Searles never include imagining sexual intercourse (or any other explicit sexual activity) with the patient. I believe that this quality of Searles' fantasies reflects the nature of the conscious and unconscious fantasy life of the oedipal child. Although drawing this parallel between the analytic experience and the childhood experience is left largely to the reader, it seems to me that Searles is suggesting that for the oedipal boy, the idea of "marrying" his mother and being her "husband" are mysterious, ill-defined and exciting ideas. To "marry" one's mother/patient is not so much a matter of having her as a sexual partner as it is a matter of having her all to oneself for one's entire life, having her as one's best friend and one's very beautiful, sexually exciting "wife" whom one deeply loves and feels deeply loved by. Searles' writing does not make it clear to what degree these feelings and fantasies are conscious to Searles (or, by extension, to the oedipal child); that unclarity is, I believe, fully intended and reflects an aspect of the quality of Searles' (and perhaps the oedipal child's) emotional state while in the grips of oedipal love.

In this first clinical example, Searles describes feeling anxious, guilty and embarrassed by his love for his patient. In response to the patient saying that she felt sad about the imminent termination of the analysis, Searles said to her that he

felt . . . much as did Mrs. Gilbreth, of *Cheaper by the Dozen* fame, [who] . . . said to her husband, when the youngest of their twelve children was now passing out of the phase of early infancy, "It

159

surely will be strange not to be waking up, for the first time in sixteen years, for the two-o'clock feeding!"

(p. 290)

The patient looked "startled and murmured something about thinking that she had become older than that" (p. 290). Searles, in retrospect, came to understand that his focus on the patient's infantile needs represented an anxious retreat from his feelings of love for her as "an adult woman who could never be mine" (p. 290). Searles' fear of acknowledging to himself and (indirectly) to the patient his oedipal love (as opposed to the love of a parent for his or her infant) stemmed primarily from his fear that openly acknowledging such feelings would elicit attacks from his external and internal analytic elders:

> My training had been predominantly such as to make me hold rather suspect any strong feelings on the part of the analyst towards his patient, and these particular emotions [romantic and erotic wishes to marry the patient] seemed to be of an especially illegitimate nature.
>
> (p. 285)

Searles, even in this only partially successful management of oedipal love in the analytic setting, is implicitly raising an important question regarding his own experience of oedipal love for the patient. What is countertransference love as opposed to "non-countertransference" love? Is the former less real than the latter? If so, in what way? These questions are left unresolved for the time being.

Searles, over the course of time, experienced oedipal love in the transference–countertransference as a consistent part of his analytic work. He says:

> I have grown successively less troubled at finding such responses in myself, less constrained to conceal these from the patient, and increasingly convinced that they augur well rather than ill for the outcome of our relationship, and that the patient's self-esteem benefits greatly from his sensing that he (or she) is capable of arousing such responses in his analyst. I have come to believe that there is a direct correlation between, on the one hand, the *affective intensity* with which the analyst experiences an awareness of such feelings – and of the unrealizability of such feelings – in himself

towards the patient, and, on the other hand, the depth of maturation which the patient achieves in the analysis.

(p. 291)

This passage illustrates the power of understatement in Searles' work. He leaves unspoken the central idea of the paper: *in order to successfully analyze the Oedipus complex, the analyst must fall in love with the patient while recognizing that his wishes will never be realized.* And, by extension, a successful oedipal experience in childhood requires that the oedipal parent fall deeply in love with the oedipal child while remaining fully aware that this love will never leave the domain of feelings. (In passages such as the one just cited, Searles seamlessly generates clinical theory from clinical description of the transference–countertransference.)

Searles' presentation of this first clinical example suggests an essential paradox underlying healthy oedipal love: both in childhood and in the transference–countertransference, the wished-for marriage is treated simultaneously as a real and as an imaginary marriage. There is at once the belief that the marriage is possible, and yet, at the same time, the knowledge (secured by the parents'/analyst's groundedness in their roles as parents/analyst) that the marriage is never to be. In the spirit of Winnicott's (1951) conception of transitional object relatedness, the question, "Does the analyst *really* want to marry his patient?" is never raised. The oedipal love of the patient and the analyst involves a state of mind suspended between reality and fantasy (see Gabbard, 1996, for a thoughtful examination and elaboration of this conception of transference–countertransference love).

The clinical examples that Searles provides in the remainder of his paper are all taken from work with chronic schizophrenic patients. Searles believes, on the basis of his extensive psychotherapeutic work at Chestnut Lodge, that the analysis of schizophrenic patients (and other patients suffering from psychological illnesses that have their origins in very early life) affords a particularly fruitful way of learning about the nature of experience that is common to all humankind. Searles also believes that successful analytic work with such patients leads to an analytic relationship in which the most mature aspects of development (including the resolution of the Oedipus complex) are not only experienced and verbalized, but have a clarity and intensity, both in the transference and the countertransference, that is rare in work with healthier patients.

In discussing the analysis of a schizophrenic woman, Searles acknowledges that it was disconcerting to him, late in that analysis, to find himself feeling strong wishes to marry a woman "whom one's fellows might perceive as being . . . grossly ill and anything but attractive" (p. 292). But Searles' capacity to see his patient as a beautiful, highly desirable woman is precisely what was required of him. Searles found that straightforwardly facing his romantic feelings for this schizophrenic patient (while remaining clear in his own mind that he was the therapist) contributed to

> the resolution of what had become a stereotyped situation of the patient's being absorbed in making incestuous appeals to, or demands upon, the therapist, in a fashion which had been throttling the mutual investigation of the patient's difficulties . . . [W]hen . . . a therapist dare not even recognize such responses in himself – let alone expressing them to the patient – the situation tends all the more to remain stalemated at this level.
>
> (pp. 292–293)

killing

Searles is suggesting here that the therapist "candidly" (p. 292) allowing the patient to see that he or she stirs in him wishes to marry the patient does not have the effect of exacerbating the patient's unrelenting "incestuous appeals"; rather, the therapist's acknowledgement of "romantic love for the patient" contributes to the "resolution" of the stalemate (the repetitive, unrelenting incestuous appeals) and the "freeing-up" (p. 292) of the patient's and the therapist's capacities for analytic work. Though Searles does not discuss the theoretical underpinnings of his findings, it seems that the therapeutic effect of the expression of the therapist's love for the patient is not being conceptualized as a corrective emotional experience, but as the meeting of a developmental need for recognition of who the patient is (as opposed to the satisfying of an erotic desire). The latter would lead to increased sexual excitement; the former fosters psychological maturation, including the consolidation of a self that is experienced as both loved and loving. Searles is implicitly, and only implicitly, positing a human developmental need to love and be loved and to be recognized as a separate person whose love is valued.

Searles deepens his investigation into the role of the analyst's feelings of oedipal love for the patient by discussing a complex emotional situation that came to a head about 18 months into the analysis of a

162

"sensitive, highly intelligent, physically handsome" (p. 294) paranoid schizophrenic man. Searles began to feel uneasy about the intensity of his feelings for this patient. He says he became alarmed during a session

> while we were sitting in silence and a radio not far away was playing a tenderly romantic song, when I realized that this man was dearer to me than anyone else in the world, including my wife. Within a few months I succeeded in finding 'reality' reasons why I would not be able to continue indefinitely with his therapy, and he moved to a distant part of the country.
>
> (p. 294)

Searles hypothesizes that he had been able to tolerate the patient's sarcasm and scorn which replicated in the transference the patient's experience of feeling hated by his mother and, in return, feeling hateful toward her. What Searles had been unable "to brave" (p. 295) was the love in the transference–countertransference which had its origins in the love that had "prevailed [between the patient and his mother] behind a screen of mutual rejection" (p. 295). In particular, it was his romantic love for a man that frightened Searles so profoundly, at that early point in his career, that he was unable to continue working with this patient.

Searles' description of sitting with this patient while a radio was playing a tender love song never fails to stir me deeply. Searles does not simply tell the reader what occurred; he shows the reader what happened in the experience of reading: the tenderness of the music is created in the sound of the words. In the sentence describing this experience (cited above), the words "while we were" (three mono-syllabic words repeating the soft "w" sound) are followed by "sitting in silence" (a pairing of two-syllable words beginning with a soft, sensuous "s" sound). The sentence continues to echo the soft "w's" of "while we were" in the words "away," "was," and "when," and ends with three tagged-on words which explode like a hand grenade: "including my wife." (At the core of the denouement is the word "wife," which, with its own soft "w," conveys the feeling that this is the word that has been adumbrated all along, the word that has lain in wait in all that has preceded. The easy movement of sound creates in the experience of reading the tranquility of the love that Searles and the patient felt for one another, while the tagged-on thought, "including my wife," powerfully cuts through the dreamy quietude of the scene.

In this way, Searles creates in the experience of reading something of his experience of sudden, unexpected alarm at the juncture of the analysis being presented. The reader, too, is unprepared for this development and wonders if Searles could *really* mean what he says: that the patient felt more dear to him than his wife. The compactness of the phrase "including my wife" contributes to the unequivocal nature of the answer to this question: yes, he does mean it. And that fact so frightened Searles that he precipitated the premature end of the therapy. I believe that alarming surprises to the reader such as the one just described account for a good deal of the intense anger Searles was notorious for eliciting from audiences to whom he presented his work. Searles refuses to round the edges of an experience. Reading his work is not an experience of arriving at an understanding; it is an experience of being rudely woken up to disconcerting truths about one's experience with one's patients. Successive experiences of "waking up" to oneself, on the part of both patient and analyst, for Searles, are pivotal aspects of the analytic experience. It is when the therapist is not able to wake up to what is occurring that acting in and acting out (on the part of both the patient and analyst) tend to occur. Here, too, these bits of clinical theory are implicit in Searles' descriptions of his clinical work.

In another analytic experience involving oedipal love for a man (which occurred some years after the clinical experience just described), Searles speaks of feeling a mixture of tender love and murderous hatred toward a severely ill paranoid schizophrenic man:

> He referred to us, now in the third and fourth years of analysis, as being married . . . When I took him for a ride in my car for one of the sessions, I was amazed at the wholly delightful fantasy and feeling I had, namely that we were lovers on the threshold of marriage, with a whole world of wonders opening up before us; I had visions of going . . . to look for furniture together.
>
> (p. 295)

The final detail of "going . . . to look for furniture together" poignantly conveys the excitement not of sexual arousal, but of dreaming and planning a life to be lived with the person one loves. In oedipal love, these dreams on the part of both child and parent, patient and analyst, cannot be lived out with the current object of one's love: "I was filled with a poignant realization of how utterly and tragically unrealizable were the desires of this man who had been hospitalized continually, now, for fourteen years" (p. 296). In this second example of oedipal love for a man, Searles is saddened, not frightened, by his love for the patient. By this point in the paper, it comes as a surprise to me, but not as a shock, that Searles took for a ride in his car a patient for whom he was experiencing feelings of love and fantasies of being married. In reading this passage, I feel "amazed" (p. 295), to use Searles' word, not shocked or horrified, by Searles' capacity to invent psychoanalysis anew for this patient (see Ogden, 2004a, 2005c). Not only has Searles grown emotionally in the course of the work that he has presented to this point, but perhaps I, too, as reader, have matured in the course of the experience of reading his work.

For me, the paper builds toward a moment near its end when Searles speaks of his own experience as a parent and as a husband. I will quote this passage in its entirety because no paraphrase, no set of excerpts can convey the effect created by the force of Searles' carefully chosen words:

> Not only my work with patients but also my experiences as a husband and a parent have convinced me of the validity of the current concepts which I am offering here. Towards my daughter, now eight years of age, I have experienced innumerable fantasies and feelings of a romantic-love kind, thoroughly complementary to the romantically adoring, seductive behaviour which she has shown towards her father oftentimes ever since she was about two or three years of age. I used at times to feel somewhat worried when she would play the supremely confident coquette with me and I would feel enthralled by her charms; but then I came to the conviction, some time ago, that such moments of relatedness could only be nourishing for her developing personality as well as delightful to me. If a little girl cannot feel herself able to win the heart of her father, her own father who has known her so well and for so long, and who is tied to her by mutual blood-ties, I reasoned, then how can the young woman who comes later have any deep confidence in the power of her womanliness?
>
> And I have every impression, similarly, that the oedipal desires of my son, now eleven years of age, have found a similarly lively and wholehearted feeling-response in my wife; and I am equally

convinced that their deeply fond, openly evidenced mutual attraction is good for my son as well as enriching to my wife. To me it *makes sense* that the more a woman loves her husband, the more she will love, similarly, the lad who is, to at least a considerable degree, the younger edition of the man she loved enough to marry.

(p. 296, my italics)

In this passage, Searles simply states, on the basis of his experience, what "makes sense" to him about the emotional effects that people have on one another. Simply saying what "makes sense" on the basis of one's experience – I cannot think of a better way of conveying the essential core of Searles' analytic thinking and way of practising psychoanalysis.

The movement of the paper as a whole, and of this passage in particular, has the feel of a succession of photographs, each more skillfully crafted, each more successful in capturing the core of the subject being photographed: the analytic relationship. The words and images that are most alive for me in this passage – words and images that often come to my mind during analytic sessions – are the ones that Searles uses to describe the way his daughter, as a small child, could wrap him around her little finger: "If a little girl cannot feel herself able to win the heart of her father, . . . then how can the young woman who comes later have any deep conviction in the power of her womanliness?" (p. 296). But even as his daughter is sweeping him off his feet, Searles' wife, who earlier had stood in the shadows of his love for one of his patients, now takes her place in the mutual feeling of love that she and Searles experience, which is the source of the oedipal love that they feel for their children. In the very experience of writing and reading the paper, there is a movement from the experience of being enthralled with the person one (oedipally) loves to the "restitution" (Loewald, 1979, p. 393) of the parents' adult love for one another as the ballast for the oedipal experience (see Chapter 8).

As Searles' paper proceeds, the reader becomes increasingly aware of differences between Freud's (explicit) and Searles' (largely implicit) conceptions of the Oedipus complex. Searles points out that in Freud's (1900) earliest description of the Oedipus complex (in *The Interpretation of Dreams*), he "makes a fuller acknowledgement of the parents' participation in the oedipal phase of the child" (p. 297) than he does in any of his subsequent writings:

166

The parents too give evidence as a rule of sexual partiality: a natural predilection usually sees to it that a man tends to spoil his little daughters while his wife takes her sons' part.

(Freud, 1900, pp. 257–258; cited in Searles, 1959, p. 297)

Even this statement of the parents' oedipal love for the child is a pale rendering of what, in Searles' hands, is a vibrant, living thing which constitutes a good deal of the richness of human life, both for children and for parents. But this is not the heart of the difference between Searles' and Freud's conceptions of the Oedipus complex. For Freud (1910, 1921, 1923, 1924, 1925), the story of the healthy Oedipus complex is that of the child's triangulated sexual desire and romantic love for one parent, and his jealousy, intense rivalry and murderous wishes for the other parent; the child's fearful and guilty renunciation (in the face of castration threats) of his sexual and romantic desires toward his parents; and the internalization of the threatening, punitive oedipal parents in the process of superego formation.

By contrast, Searles' version of the Oedipus complex is the story of the child's experience of reciprocated romantic and sexual love of the parent (a wish "to marry" and make a family and home with that parent). There is rivalry with, and jealousy of, the other parent, but it is a far quieter affair than that involved in Freud's conception of the child's murderous wishes for his parents. Searles' version of the oedipal experience does not end with the child feeling defeated by castration threats and being left with an abiding sense of guilt and the need to renounce and ashamedly hide sexual and romantic wishes for the parent.

Instead, for Searles, the healthy Oedipus complex is the story of love and loss, of reciprocated romantic parent–child love that is safeguarded by the parents' firm but compassionate recognition of their roles both as parents and as a couple. That recognition on the part of the parents helps the child (and the parents themselves) to accept the fact that this intense parent–child love relationship must be given up:

The renunciation is, I think, again [like the reciprocation of the child's oedipal love] something which is a mutual experience for child and parent, and is made in deference to a recognizedly greater limiting reality, a reality which includes not only the taboo maintained by the rival-parent, but also the love of the oedipally desired parent towards his or her spouse – a love which antedated the child's birth and the love to which, in a sense, he owes his very existence.

(p. 302)

In this rendering of the Oedipus complex, the child emerges with a feeling that his romantic and sexual love is accepted, valued and reciprocated, along with a firm recognition of a "greater limiting reality" within which he must live. Both elements – the love and the loss – strengthen the child psychologically. The first element – the reciprocated oedipal love – enhances the child's self-esteem. The second element – the loss involved in the waning of the oedipal romance – contributes to the child's sense of "a recognizedly greater limiting reality" (p. 302). This sense of a greater limiting reality involves an enhancement of the child's capacity to recognize and accept the unrealizability of his desires. This maturational step has far more to do with the maturation of reality testing and the capacity to differentiate internal and external reality than with the internalization of a chastising, threatening, punitive version of the parents (that is, superego formation). For Searles, the "heir" to the Oedipus complex is not primarily the formation of the superego, but a sense of oneself as a loving and lovable person who recognizes (with a feeling of loss) the constraints of external reality.

We can hear in this passage a partial response to the question raised earlier: "Is countertransference love, for Searles, less real than other kinds of love?" Clearly the answer is no. What makes countertransference love different from other types of love is the analyst's responsibility to recognize that the love that he experiences for and from the patient is an aspect of the analytic relationship and to make use of it in the therapeutic work in which he is engaged with the patient:

These feelings [of love for the patient] come to him [the analyst] like all feelings, without tags showing whence they have come, and only if he is relatively open and accepting of their emergence into his awareness does he have a chance to set about finding out . . . their significance in his work with the patient.

(pp. 300–301)

The notion that feelings come to the analyst "without tags" is pivotal to Searles' conception of oedipal love in the countertransference and to his overall conception of psychoanalysis. The analyst's task is first and foremost to allow himself to experience the full emotional intensity of *all that he feels in the here-and-now of the analytic experience.* Only then is he in a position to make analytic use of his feeling state.

Unconscious identification

I will now turn to Searles' "Unconscious identification" (1990), an important but little known paper published in a collection of papers by 14 analysts more than three decades after the "Oedipal love" paper was published. The later paper reveals Searles' clinical thinking in its most highly developed form. There can be no doubt that the speaker in Searles' 1990 paper is the same person as the speaker in the 1959 paper, but now wiser, more artful in his work, more keenly aware of his limitations. In his 1990 paper, Searles is even more spare in his use of psychoanalytic theory than he was in the "Oedipal love" paper. So far as I am able to discern, in his 1990 paper, Searles makes use of only two analytic theories: the concept of the dynamic unconscious and the concept of the transference–countertransference. The effect of Searles' paring away of theory to its absolute minimum is the creation of an experience in reading that is akin to that of reading fine literature: emotional situations and the characters involved in these situations are allowed to speak for themselves.

Searles begins the paper with a metaphor:

> My main purpose in this chapter is to convey a generous variety of clinical vignettes wherein one can detect unconscious identifications ramifying beneath or behind a relatively simple and obvious conscious one, something like a sea plant can be discovered to be flourishing far beyond and beneath the few leaves that can be seen on the water's surface.
>
> (1990, p. 211)

Searles lays out in this opening sentence his conception of how he views the relationship of conscious and unconscious experience in the analytic relationship. Conscious experience is "relatively simple and obvious," if one has developed an ear with which to notice it in oneself and frame it for oneself; "beneath or behind" conscious experience is unconscious experience which is continuous with conscious

169

experience, just as the "flourishing," "ramifying" underwater parts of the sea plant are continuous with "the few leaves that can be seen at the water's surface." Implicit in this metaphor, as I read it, is the idea that one need not be a marine biologist to notice a few of the qualities of the sea plant, but the more one's mind and senses are capable of refined perception, the more one is likely to understand about the way the plant works and how it has come to work in that way. Moreover, a person with a trained eye is also more likely to feel curious, puzzled and amazed by what he observes. And yet, as I hope to show in the course of my discussion of this paper, Searles' use of this metaphor fails to capture what is most important about his way of thinking and working.

In the first of the clinical illustrations, Searles describes his work with an elderly woman who for many years had not heard from her daughter. Having received a letter from her daughter (then in her forties), the patient brought the letter to the session, not certain how to reply to it. She gave it to Searles to read. On thinking about it, Searles said, "I do feel a sense of not actually being you, and therefore, I feel uncomfortable as to how I might respond to it" (p. 214). A bit later, Searles conversationally addresses the reader:

> Actually, for me, the most memorable aspect of this interaction is that, in the moment before reaching out to accept the letter, I felt a very strong sense that it was not right for me to read the letter, since *I* was not the person to whom the letter was addressed; the force of this inhibition was striking to me, in light of her obvious wish that I read it.
>
> It then occurred to me, as I went on talking, and I said, "But I wonder if *you* feel that *you*, likewise, are not the person to whom that letter is addressed." To this, she reacted in a strongly confirmatory fashion, saying that she had gotten a great deal of therapy over the years since she had been involved in the kind of thing that this letter was expressing. In essence, she strongly confirmed that my sense of not in actuality being the intended recipient of the letter had a counterpart in her strongly feeling, likewise, that she was not the person to whom the letter was addressed. Her confirmation, here, was expressed in sufficiently pent-up feeling as to let me know that she had needed this interpretation from me to enable her to know and express these feelings so clearly.
>
> (pp. 214–215)

The analytic event being presented hinges on Searles' awareness in the moment before he reached out to accept the letter that he felt uncomfortable with the idea of reading a letter that was not written to him. On the basis of this feeling/thought, Searles did something with the situation that, for me, is astounding: he turned the experience "inside out" in his mind in a way that revealed something that felt true to him, to the patient, and to me, as a reader. (With regard to my use of the metaphor of turning experience inside out, it is important to bear in mind that, like the surface of a Moebius strip, inside is continually in the process of becoming outside and outside becoming inside.) Searles took his feeling that it was not right to read a letter not addressed to him – the "inside," in the sense that it was his own personal response – and made it "the outside." By "outside," I mean the context, the larger emotional reality, within which he was experiencing what was occurring between himself and the patient, and, by extension, within which the patient was experiencing herself in relation to her daughter. It is precisely this sort of reversal that is most surprising, often startling, about the experience of reading Searles: there is an abrupt shift from Searles' inner life (his extraordinarily perceptive emotional response to what is occurring) to the invisible psychological context within which the patient is experiencing himself or herself.

It is important to note that the reversal to which I am referring is not synonymous with making the unconscious conscious. What Searles does is far more subtle than that. In this example, the patient's experience of no longer being the person her daughter imagines her to be is not a repressed unconscious thought and feeling; rather, it is part of the internal emotional environment in which the patient lives. That as yet unnamed matrix of her self had come to constitute a good deal of the truth of who she had become. In the interaction described, it was necessary, first, for Searles to make a transformation within himself in which context became content, the "invisible" context of Searles' sense of himself (as not being the person to whom the letter was written), became the "visible," thinkable content. Searles, in the process of thinking out loud, came to the feeling/ idea that the patient did not experience herself as the person to whom the letter was written: "It then occurred to me, as I went on talking . . ." (p. 214). Searles was not saying what he thought; he was thinking what he said. That is, in the very act of speaking, inner was becoming outer, thinking was becoming talking, unthinkable context was becoming thinkable content, experience was being turned inside out.

I will now turn to another example of Searles turning experience inside out. In a clinical discussion later in the paper, he recounts instances of being asked by patients, "How are you?" Searles describes often feeling

> that I would dearly love to be able to unburden myself, and tell him in . . . detail of the myriad aspects of how I am feeling today; but knowing how impossible this is, in light of our true situation here, I react mainly with bitterly ironic amusement saying, "Just grand," or merely nodding.
>
> (p. 216)

It eventually occurs to Searles, each time freshly and unexpectedly, that the patient is feeling something very similar to Searles' feelings, i.e. that it is impossible under the circumstances to tell Searles how he (the patient) feels. This is so because "*he* [the patient] is [feeling that he is] supposed to be the one who is helping *me*" (p. 216) as was the case in the patient's childhood relationship with his parents. When Searles comes to this type of understanding of the situation, he remains silent and yet his grasp of what is occurring "nonetheless enables me . . . to foster an atmosphere wherein the patient can feel that he is being met with more of genuine patience and empathy than had been the case before" (p. 216).

In this clinical situation, Searles realizes that a critical aspect of the context of his emotional experience of being the analyst for his patient has been his (Searles') wish to be the patient in the analysis. His hearing the bitterness in his own voice as he responds to the patient's question/invitation makes it possible for him to convert unthinkable context into thinkable content. This transformation allows Searles to communicate (nonverbally) an understanding of the patient's invisible (silent) bitterness about the fact that he does not feel that he has the right to be the patient in his own analysis. Here, again, Searles does the psychological work of transforming his own "inner" emotional context (his wish that the analysis were his own analysis) into "outer" (thinkable, verbally symbolized) thoughts and feelings. This psychological work on Searles' part contributes to a change in the "atmosphere" of the analytic relationship. The formerly unthinkable context for the patient's experience (his sense that the

172

analysis was not *his* analysis) enters a process of being consciously thought by Searles and unconsciously thought by the patient.

I will take a piece of Searles' self-analytic work as a final illustration of the way in which his thinking is, to a great extent, marked by his unique way of turning experience inside out:

> For many years I have enjoyed washing dishes, and not rarely have had the feeling that this is the one thing in my life that I feel entirely comfortably capable of doing. I have always assumed that, in my washing of dishes, I was identifying with my mother, who routinely did them in my early childhood. But in recent years . . . it has occurred to me that I have been identifying with my mother not only in the form but also in my spirit of washing the dishes. I had not previously allowed myself to consider the possibility that she, too, may have felt so chronically overwhelmed, so chronically out beyond her depth in life, that this activity, this washing of dishes, was the one part of her life with which she felt fully equipped to cope comfortably.
>
> (p. 224)

This paragraph could have been written by no one other than Searles – in part because it involves such exquisite mastery of the art of looking deeply *into* seemingly ordinary conscious experience. Searles knows in a way that few analysts have known that there is only one consciousness and that the unconscious aspect of consciousness is *in* the conscious aspect, not under it or behind it. Paradoxically, Searles knows this in practice and makes use of it in virtually every clinical illustration he presents, but he has not, as far as I am aware, ever discussed this conception of consciousness in his writing. Moreover, in the opening sentence of the paper cited earlier, Searles explicitly contradicts this understanding of the relationship of conscious and unconscious experience when he says that unconscious identifications lie "behind and beneath" conscious identifications. I believe, however, that this conception of the relationship between conscious and unconscious experience (and the accompanying sea plant metaphor) are not in keeping with the understanding of the relationship between conscious and unconscious experience that Searles so powerfully illustrates in this paper. I believe that it would more accurately reflect what Searles demonstrates in his clinical work to say that conscious and unconscious experience are qualities of a unitary

173

consciousness and that we gain access to the unconscious dimension of experience by looking *into* conscious experience, not by looking "behind" it or "beneath" it.

In the account of his psychological state while washing dishes, Searles had for years thought of his enjoyment of washing dishes and his feeling that that is the "one thing in my life that I feel entirely comfortably capable of doing," as an identification in the "form," but not in the "spirit" of his mother washing dishes. The reader (and Searles) are taken by surprise as Searles delves more deeply into his experience of washing dishes. He becomes aware of what he already "knew," but did not know: his experience of washing dishes takes place within a powerful, yet invisible emotional context of feelings of profound inadequacy. Searles transforms this formerly unthinkable context into thinkable emotional content: "I had not previously allowed myself to consider the possibility that she, too, may have felt so chronically overwhelmed, so chronically out beyond her depth in life, that this activity, this washing of dishes, was the one part of her life with which she felt fully equipped to cope comfortably" (p. 224). The truth (and even beauty) of Searles' newly created understanding of himself and his mother is not merely described for the reader, it is shown to the reader in the evocativeness of the imagery. The image of Searles as a child watching his mother with a sink full of dishes in soapy water not only captures the experience of the day-to-day life of a boy with his depressed mother; it also conveys a sense of the emotional shallowness (the very limited depth of a kitchen sink) beyond which his mother dared not – could not – go.

Searles and Bion

I will conclude this paper by briefly discussing a complementarity between Searles' thinking and that of Bion which I "discovered" to my surprise in the course of writing this paper. Searles was temperamentally disinclined (and perhaps unable) to formulate his thoughts at a level of abstraction beyond that of clinical theory. In stark contrast, Bion, whose focus was on the development of psychoanalytic theory, gives the reader very little sense of the way in which he makes use of his ideas in the analytic setting. In a highly condensed way, I will address three aspects of the work of Searles and Bion in

174

which I suggest that the reader requires familiarity with the work of both authors in order to fully appreciate either one.

The container–contained

In discussing Searles' way of working with his patient's request that he read a letter written to her by her daughter, I introduced the idea that Searles' thinking might be thought of as "turning experience inside out" – what begins as the invisible, unthinkable context of experience is transformed by Searles into experiential content, about which he and the patient may be able to think and talk. My metaphoric description of what Searles was doing (without my being aware of it) drew on Bion's (1962a) concept of the container–contained. The concept of the container–contained provides a way of thinking about the way in which psychological content (thoughts and feelings) may overwhelm and destroy the very capacity for thinking thoughts (the container) (see Ogden, 2004b, for a discussion of Bion's concept of the container–contained). Searles' patient may have harbored feelings of guilt of such intensity that they limited her capacity to think her thoughts concerning the ways in which she had changed, thus leaving her without the means to do unconscious psychological work with them. Searles was able to think (contain) something like the patient's unthinkable thoughts concerning his own guilt/uneasiness about the idea of reading a letter not addressed to him. In telling the patient that he thought that she, too, did not experience herself as the person to whom the letter was written, Searles helped the patient to contain/think her own previously unthinkable thoughts and feelings concerning the psychological growth that she had achieved.

In formulating Searles' work in this way, I am creating a vantage point that is lacking in Searles' work, i.e. a conception of the way in which the analytic interaction involves at every turn the muscular interplay of thoughts and the capacity to think one's thoughts. At the same time, Searles' extraordinary capacity to describe the emotional shifts occurring in the transference–countertransference brings to life the experiential level of the workings of the container–contained in ways that, to my mind, Bion was unable to achieve in his own writing.

175

Strong

The human need for truth

Searing honesty (with himself and with the patient) permeates Searles' accounts of his clinical work. Examples previously discussed in this paper that come immediately to mind include Searles' acknowledging to himself (despite internal and external pressures to do otherwise) his intense wishes to marry his patients when in the thick of oedipal transference–countertransference experiences; Searles' alarming awareness that he felt a depth of tenderness toward a male schizophrenic patient that was greater than the love he felt for his wife; and his recognition of his feelings of bitterness about the fact that he was not the patient in the analysis that he was conducting and, consequently, did not have the right to tell the patient at length what he was feeling. While Searles clearly believes that straightforwardly facing the truth of what is occurring in the analytic relationship is an indispensable element in analytic work, it took Bion to formulate this clinical awareness at a higher level of abstraction, namely, that the most fundamental principle of human motivation is the need to know the truth about one's lived emotional experience. "[T]he welfare of the patient demands a constant supply of truth as inevitably as his physical survival demands food" (Bion, 1992, p. 99). Searles is without peer in demonstrating what that need for truth looks like and feels like in the transference–countertransference and how it shapes the analytic experience; Bion put the idea into words, located it in relation to analytic theory as a whole, and created an understanding of the human condition that placed the need for truth at its core.

Reconceiving the relationship between conscious and unconscious experience

It is evident in Searles' description of his analytic work that the relationship between the analyst's conscious and unconscious experience is being conceived of quite differently from the way in which that interplay is ordinarily thought of. Though he does not state it explicitly, Searles shows the reader what it means to make use of consciousness as a whole – that is, to create conditions in the analytic setting in which the analyst perceives what is occurring in the transference–countertransference by means of a form of consciousness characterized by a seamless continuity of conscious and unconscious experience. Bion recognized in his own work what Searles demonstrates in his clinical accounts, and used that recognition to revolutionize analytic theory by radically altering the topographic model. Bion's alteration of the topographic model is nothing less than breathtaking in that it had been impossible, at least for me, to imagine psychoanalysis without the idea of an unconscious mind somehow separate from ("below") the conscious mind. The conscious and unconscious "minds," for Bion, are not separate entities, but dimensions of a single consciousness. The apparent separateness of the conscious and unconscious parts of the mind is, for Bion (1962a), merely an artifact of the vantage point from which we observe and think about human experience. In other words, consciousness and unconsciousness are aspects of a single entity viewed from different vertices (see Ogden, 2004a). The unconscious is always a dimension of consciousness whether or not it is easily perceptible, just as the stars are always in the sky whether or not they are obscured by the glare of the sun.

Bion (1962a) developed his concept of "reverie" (a state of receptivity to one's own and the patient's conscious/unconscious experience) concurrently with Searles' early descriptions (written in the 1950s and 1960s) of his work with chronic schizophrenic patients in which he makes use of a state of mind that blurs the distinction between conscious and unconscious aspects of experience. It is impossible to say to what extent Bion was influenced by Searles or Searles by Bion. Searles makes reference only to Bion's relatively early work on projective identification; Bion makes no reference at all to Searles' work. Nonetheless, what I hope to have demonstrated is that Searles' work is enriched conceptually by a knowledge of Bion's work and Bion's work is brought more fully to life experientially by a familiarity with Searles' work.

References

Barros, E. and Barros, E. (2009). Reflections on the clinical implications of symbolism in dream life. Presented to the São Paulo Psychoanalytic Society, 8 August 2009.

Bellow, S. (2000). *Ravelstein*. New York: Penguin.

Bion, W. R. (1957). Differentiation of the psychotic from the non-psychotic parts of the personality. In *Second Thoughts*. New York: Aronson, 1967 (pp. 93–109).

Bion, W. R. (1959). Attacks on linking. *International Journal of Psychoanalysis* 40: 308–315.

Bion, W. R. (1962a). *Learning From Experience*. New York: Basic Books.

Bion, W. R. (1962b). A theory of thinking. In *Second Thoughts*. New York: Aronson (pp. 110–119).

Bion, W. R. (1963). *Elements of Psycho-Analysis*. In *Seven Servants*. New York: Jason Aronson, 1977.

Bion, W. R. (1967). Notes on the theory of schizophrenia. In *Second Thoughts*. New York: Aronson (pp. 23–35).

Bion, W. R. (1970). *Attention and Interpretation*. In *Seven Servants*. New York: Aronson.

Bion, W. R. (1975). Brasilia clinical seminars. In *Clinical Seminars and Four Papers*. Abingdon, England: Fleetwood Press, 1987 (pp. 1–118).

Bion, W. R. (1976). On a quotation from Freud. In *Clinical Seminars and Four Papers*. Abingdon, England: Fleetwood Press, 1987 (pp. 234–238).

Bion, W. R. (1978). São Paulo clinical seminars. In *Clinical Seminars and Four Papers*. Abingdon, England: Fleetwood Press, 1987 (pp. 121–220).

Bion, W. R. (1982). *The Long Week-end, 1987–1919*. Abingdon, England: Fleetwood Press, 1982.

Bion, W. R. (1987). Clinical seminars. In F. Bion (ed.) *Clinical Seminars and Other Works*. London: Karnac (pp. 1–240).

Bion, W. R. (1992). *Cogitations* (F. Bion, ed.). London: Karnac.

178

References

Borges, J. L. (1923). Foreword. In *Jorge Luis Borges: Selected Poems, 1923–1967* (N. T. Di Giovanni, ed. and trans.). New York: Dell, 1972 (p. 269).

Borges, J. L. (1944). *Ficciones [Fictions]*. Buenos Aires, Argentina: Editorial Sud.

Borges, J. L. (1957). Borges and I. In *Labyrinths: Selected Stories and Other Writings* (J. Irby and P. A. Yates, eds; J. Irby, trans.). New York: New Directions, 1962 (pp. 246–247).

Borges, J. L. (1962). Kafka and his precursors. In *Labyrinths: Selected Stories and Other Writings* (J. Irby and P. A. Yates, eds; J. Irby, trans.). New York: New Directions (pp. 199–201).

Borges, J. L. (1984). *Twenty-Four Conversations with Borges: Interviews with Roberto Alifano, 1981–1983 (Including a Selection of Poems)* (N. S. Arauz, W. Barnstone, and N. Escandell, trans.). Housatonic, MA: Lascoux.

Bornstein, M. (1975). Qualities of color vision in infancy. *Journal of Experimental Child Psychology* 19: 401–419.

Breuer, J. and Freud, S. (1893–1895). *Studies on Hysteria*. SE 2.

Cambray, J. (2002). Synchronicity and emergence. *American Imago* 59: 409–434.

Chodorow, N. (2003). The psychoanalytic vision of Hans Loewald. *International Journal of Psychoanalysis* 84: 897–913.

Chomsky, N. (1957). *Syntactic Structures*. The Hague: Mouton.

Chomsky, N. (1968). *Language and Mind*. New York: Harcourt, Brace and World.

Emerson, E. (1841). Spiritual laws. In *The Essays of Ralph Waldo Emerson*. Cambridge, MA: Belknap Press, 1987 (pp. 75–96).

Fairbairn, W. R. D. (1940). Schizoid factors in the personality. In *Psychoanalytic Studies of the Personality*. London: Routledge and Kegan Paul, 1952 (pp. 3–27).

Fairbairn, W. R. D. (1941). A revised psychopathology of the psychoses and psychoneuroses. In *Psychoanalytic Studies of the Personality*. London: Routledge and Kegan Paul, 1952 (pp. 28–58).

Fairbairn W. R. D. (1943a). The repression and the return of bad objects (with special reference to the 'war neuroses'). In *Psychoanalytic Studies of the Personality*. London: Routledge and Kegan Paul, 1952 (pp. 59–81).

Fairbairn, W. R. D. (1943b). Reply to Mrs Isaacs' "The nature and function of phantasy." In *The Freud–Klein Controversies, 1941–1945* (P. King and R. Steiner, eds) (New Library of Psychoanalysis). London: Routledge, 1991 (pp. 358–360).

Fairbairn, W. R. D. (1944). Endopsychic structure considered in terms of object-relationships. In *Psychoanalytic Studies of the Personality*. London: Routledge and Kegan Paul, 1952 (pp. 82–132).

Fairbairn, W. R. D. (1952). *Psychoanalytic Studies of the Personality*. London: Routledge and Kegan Paul.

Fairbairn, W. R. D. (1956). Freud, the psychoanalytical method and mental health. *British Journal of Medical Psychology* 30: 53–61.

Fairbairn, W. R. D. (1958). On the nature and aims of psychoanalytical treatment. *International Journal of Psychoanalysis* 39: 374–385.

Fairbairn, W. R. D. (1963). Synopsis of an object-relations theory of personality. *International Journal of Psychoanalysis* 44: 224–225.

Freud, A. (1936). *The Ego and the Mechanisms of Defense.* New York: International Universities Press, 1965.

Freud, S. (1900). *The Interpretation of Dreams.* SE 4/5.

Freud, S. (1909). Analysis of a phobia in a five-year-old. SE 10.

Freud, S. (1910). A special type of choice of object made by men (Contributions to a psychology of love I). SE 11.

Freud, S. (1914a). On the history of the psycho-analytic movement. SE 14.

Freud, S. (1914b). On narcissism: An introduction. SE 14.

Freud, S. (1915a). *Instincts and Their Vicissitudes.* SE 14.

Freud, S. (1915b). Repression. SE 14.

Freud, S. (1915c). The unconscious. SE 14.

Freud, S. (1916–17). *Introductory Lectures on Psycho-Analysis.* XXIII. SE 15/16.

Freud, S. (1917a). Mourning and melancholia. SE 14.

Freud, S. (1917b). A metapsychological supplement to the theory of dreams. SE 14.

Freud, S. (1921). *Group Psychology and the Analysis of the Ego.* SE 18.

Freud, S. (1923). *The Ego and the Id.* SE 19.

Freud, S. (1924). The dissolution of the Oedipus complex. SE 19.

Freud, S. (1925). Some psychical consequences of the anatomical distinction between the sexes. SE 19.

Frost, R. (1914). Mending wall. In *Robert Frost: Collected Poems, Prose, and Plays* (R. Poirier and M. Richardson, eds). New York: Library of America, 1995 (p. 39).

Frost, R. (1923a). The need of being versed in country things. In *Robert Frost: Collected Poems, Prose, and Plays* (R. Poirier and M. Richardson, eds). New York: Library of America, 1995 (p. 223).

Frost, R. (1923b). For once, then, something. In *Robert Frost: Collected Poems, Prose, and Plays* (R. Poirier and M. Richardson, eds). New York: Library of America, 1995 (p. 208).

Frost, R. (1939). The figure a poem makes. In *Robert Frost: Collected Poems, Prose, and Plays* (R. Poirier and M. Richardson, eds). New York: Library of America, 1995 (pp. 776–778).

Frost, R. (1942a). The most of it. In *Robert Frost: Collected Poems, Prose, and Plays* (R. Poirier and M. Richardson, eds). New York: Library of America, 1995 (p. 307).

Frost, R. (1942b). Carpe diem. In *Robert Frost: Collected Poems, Prose and Plays* (R. Poirier and M. Richardson, eds). New York: Library of America, 1995 (p. 305).

Frost, R. (1947). Directive. In *Robert Frost: Collected Poems, Prose, and Plays* (R. Poirier and M. Richardson, eds). New York: Library of America, 1995 (pp. 341–342).

Gabbard, G. O. (1996). *Love and Hate in the Analytic Setting*. Northvale, NJ: Aronson.

Gabbard, G. O. (2007). "Bound in a nutshell": Thoughts on complexity, reductionism and "infinite space." *International Journal of Psychoanalysis* 88: 559–574.

Gay, P. (1988). *Freud: A Life for our Time*. New Haven, CT: Yale University Press.

Green, A. (1983). The dead mother. In *Private Madness*. Madison, CT: International Universities Press, 1980 (pp. 178–206).

Greenberg, J. R. and Mitchell, S. A. (1983). *Object Relations in Psychoanalytic Theory*. Cambridge, MA: Harvard University Press.

Grotstein, J. S. (1994). Notes on Fairbairn's metapsychology. In *Fairbairn and the Origins of Object Relations* (J. S. Grotstein and D. B. Rinsley, eds). New York: Guilford (pp. 112–148).

Grotstein, J. S. (2000). *Who is the Dreamer who Dreams the Dream? A Study of Psychic Presences*. Hillsdale, NJ: Analytic Press.

Grotstein, J. S. (2007a). *A Beam of Intense Darkness: Wilfred Bion's Legacy to Psychoanalysis*. New York: Other Press.

Grotstein, J. S. (2007b). ". . . But at the Same Time and at Another Level . . ." *Psychoanalytic Technique in the Klein/Bion Mode: A Beginning*. London: Karnac.

Guntrip, H. (1968). *Schizoid Phenomena, Object Relations and the Self*. London: Hogarth.

Heaney, S. (1980). Feeling into words. In *Preoccupations: Selected Prose, 1968–1978*. New York: Noonday (pp. 41–60).

Isaacs, S. (1943a). The nature and function of phantasy. In *The Freud–Klein Controversies 1941–1945* (P. King and R. Steiner, eds) (The New Library of Psychoanalysis). London: Routledge, 1991 (pp. 264–321).

Isaacs, S. (1943b). Concerning the factual issues. In *The Freud–Klein controversies 1941–1945* (P. King and R. Steiner, eds) (The New Library of Psychoanalysis). London: Routledge, 1991 (pp. 458–473).

Isaacs, S. (1952). The nature and function of phantasy. In *Developments in Psycho-Analysis* (J. Rivière, ed.). London: Hogarth Press, 1952 (pp. 62–121).

Karp, G. and Berrill, M. (1981). *Development* (2nd ed.). New York: McGraw-Hill.

Kaywin, R. (1993). The theoretical contributions of Hans Loewald. *Psychoanalytic Study of the Child* 48: 99–114.

Kernberg, O. (1980). *External World and Internal Reality*. Northvale, N J: Aronson.

King, P. (1991). Biographical notes. In *The Freud–Klein Controversies 1941–1945* (P. King and R. Steiner, eds). London: Routledge, 1991 (pp. ix–xxv).

Klein, M. (1930). The importance of symbol-formation in the development of the ego. In *Contributions to Psycho-Analysis, 1921–1945*. London: Hogarth Press, 1968 (pp. 236–250).

Klein, M. (1935). A contribution to the psychogenesis of manic-depressive states. In *Contributions to Psycho-Analysis, 1921–1945*. London: Hogarth Press, 1968 (pp. 282–310).

Klein, M. (1940). Mourning and its relations to manic-depressive states. In *Contributions to Psycho-Analysis, 1921–1945*. London: Hogarth Press, 1968 (pp. 311–338).

Klein, M. (1946). Notes on some schizoid mechanisms. In *Envy and Gratitude and Other Works, 1946–1963*. New York: Delacorte Press/Seymour Laurence, 1975 (pp. 1–24).

Klein, M. (1952). Some theoretical conclusions regarding the emotional life of the infant. In *Envy and Gratitude and Other Works, 1946–1963*. New York: Delacorte Press/Seymour Laurence, 1975 (pp. 61–93).

Klein, M. (1955). On identification. In *Envy and Gratitude and Other Works, 1946–1963*. New York: Delacorte Press/Seymour Laurence, 1975 (pp. 141–175).

Kohut, H. (1971). *The Analysis of the Self*. New York: International Universities Press.

Laplanche, J. and Pontalis, J.-B. (1967). Repression. In *The Language of Psycho-Analysis* (D. N. Smith, trans.). New York: Norton, 1973 (pp. 390–394).

Loewald, H. (1978). Primary process, secondary process and language. In *Papers on Psychoanalysis*. New Haven, CT: Yale University Press, 1980 (pp. 178–206).

Loewald, H. (1979). The waning of the Oedipus complex. In *Papers on Psychoanalysis*. New Haven, CT: Yale University Press, 1980 (pp. 384–404).

Lorenz, K. (1937). *Studies in Animal and Human Behaviour, Vol. 1* (R. Martin, trans.). London: Methuen.

McLaughlin, B. P. (1992). The rise and fall of British emergentism. In *Emergence or Reduction? Essays on the Prospects of Non-Reductive Physicalism* (A. Beckermann, H. Flohr and J. Kim, eds). Berlin, NY: Walter de Gruyter.

Mitchell, S. H. (1998). From ghosts to ancestors: The psychoanalytic vision of Hans Loewald. *Psychoanalytic Dialogues* 8: 825–855.

Modell, A. H. (1968). *Object Love and Reality: An Introduction to a Psychoanalytic Theory of Object Relations*. New York: International Universities Press.

Ogden, T. H. (1983). The concept of internal object relations. *International Journal of Psychoanalysis* 64: 181–198.

Ogden, T. H. (1986). *The Matrix of the Mind: Object Relations and the Psychoanalytic Dialogue*. Northvale, N J: Aronson/London: Karnac.

Ogden, T. H. (1987). The transitional oedipal relationship in female development. *International Journal of Psychoanalysis* 68: 485–498.

Ogden, T. H. (1989). *The Primitive Edge of Experience*. Northvale, NJ: Aronson/London: Karnac.

Ogden, T. H. (1994a). The analytic third – working with intersubjective clinical facts. *International Journal of Psychoanalysis* 75: 3–20.

Ogden, T. H. (1994b). *Subjects of Analysis*. Northvale, NJ: Jason Aronson/London: Karnac.

Ogden, T. H. (1995). Analysing forms of aliveness and deadness of the transference–countertransference. *International Journal of Psychoanalysis* 76: 695–709.

Ogden, T. H. (1997). *Reverie and Interpretation: Sensing Something Human*. Northvale, NJ: Aronson/London: Karnac.

Ogden, T. H. (1999). The analytic third: An overview. In *Relational Psychoanalysis: The Emergence of a Tradition* (L. Aron and S. Mitchell, eds). Hillsdale, NJ: Analytic Press (pp. 487–492).

Ogden, T. H. (2001). *Conversations at the Frontier of Dreaming*. Northvale, NJ: Aronson/London: Karnac.

Ogden, T. H. (2003a). On not being able to dream. *International Journal of Psychoanalysis* 84: 17–30.

Ogden, T. H. (2003b). What's true and whose idea was it? *International Journal of Psychoanalysis* 84: 593–606.

Ogden, T. H. (2004a). This art of psychoanalysis: Dreaming undreamt dreams and interrupted cries. *International Journal of Psychoanalysis* 85: 857–877.

Ogden, T. H. (2004b). On holding and containing, being and dreaming. *International Journal of Psychoanalysis* 85: 1349–1364.

Ogden, T. H. (2005a). On psychoanalytic supervision. *International Journal of Psychoanalysis* 86: 15–29.

Ogden, T. H. (2005b). On psychoanalytic writing. *International Journal of Psychoanalysis* 86: 15–29.

Ogden, T. H. (2005c). *This Art of Psychoanalysis: Dreaming Undreamt Dreams and Interrupted Cries* (New Library of Psychoanalysis). London: Routledge.

Ogden, T. H. (2006). On teaching psychoanalysis. *International Journal of Psychoanalysis* 87: 1069–1085.

Ogden, T. H. (2010). On three forms of thinking: Magical thinking, dream thinking and transformative thinking. *Psychoanalytic Quarterly* 79: 317–347.

Plato (1997). *Phaedrus*. In *Plato: Complete Works* (J. M. Cooper, ed.). Indianapolis, IN: Hackett (pp. 506–556).

Rinsley, D. B. (1977). An object relations view of borderline personality. In *Borderline Personality Disorders* (P. Hartocollis, ed.). New York: International Universities Press (pp. 47–70).

Rivière, J. (1936). The genesis of psychical conflict in earliest infancy. *International Journal of Psychoanalysis* 17: 395–422.

Rivière, J. (1952). General introduction. In J. Rivière (ed.) *Developments in Psycho-Analysis*. London: Hogarth Press (pp. 1–36).

Rosenfeld, H. (1965). *Psychotic States*. New York: International Universities Press.

Sandler, J. (1976). Dreams, unconscious phantasies and 'identity of perception'. *International Review of Psychoanalysis* 3: 33–42.

Scharff, J. S. and Scharff, D. E. (1994). *Object Relations Theory and Trauma*. Northvale, N J: Aronson.

Searles, H. (1959). Oedipal love in the countertransference. In *Collected Papers on Schizophrenia and Related Subjects*. New York: International Universities Press, 1965 (pp. 284–304).

Searles, H. (1990). Unconscious identification. In *Master Clinicians: On Treating the Regressed Patient* (L. B. Boyer and P. Giovacchini, eds). Northvale, NJ: Aronson (pp. 211–226).

Segal, H. (1957). Notes on symbol formation. *International Journal of Psychoanalysis* 38: 391–397.

Spitz, R. (1965). *The First Year of Life*. New York: International Universities Press.

Steiner, R. (1991). Background to the scientific controversies. In *The Freud–Klein Controversies 1941–1945* (P. King and R. Steiner, eds). London: Routledge, 1991 (pp. 227–263).

Stoppard, T. (1999). Pragmatic theater. *The New York Review of Books, 46*(14): 8–10, 23 September.

Strachey, J. (1957). Papers on metapsychology: Editor's introduction. SE 14.

Sutherland, J. D. (1989). *Fairbairn's Journey into the Interior*. London: Free Associations.

Symington, N. (1986). Fairbairn. In *The Analytic Experience*. London: Free Associations (pp. 236–253).

Tinbergen, N. (1957). On anti-predator response in certain birds: A reply. *Journal of Comparative Physiologic Psychology* 50: 412–414.

Tower, L. E. (1956). Countertransference. *Journal of the American Psychoanalytical Association* 4: 224–255.

Tresan, D. (1996). Jungian metapsychology and neurobiological theory. *Journal of Analytical Psychology* 41: 399–436.

Trilling, L. (1947). Freud and literature. In *The Liberal Imagination*. New York: Anchor, 1953 (pp. 32–54).

Vargas Llosa, M. (2008). The fictions of Borges. In *Wellsprings*. Cambridge, MA: Harvard University Press (pp. 26–46).

Winnicott, D. W. (1945). Primitive emotional development. In *Through Paediatrics to Psycho-Analysis*. New York: Basic Books, 1958 (pp. 145–156).

Winnicott, D. W. (1949). Mind and its relation to the psyche-soma. In *Through Paediatrics to Psycho-Analysis*. New York: Basic Books, 1958 (pp. 243–254).

Winnicott, D. W. (1951). Transitional objects and transitional phenomena. In *Playing and Reality*. New York: Basic Books, 1971 (pp. 1–25).

Winnicott, D. W. (1956). Primary maternal preoccupation. In *Through Paediatrics to Psycho-Analysis*. New York: International Universities Press, 1975 (pp. 300–305).

Winnicott, D. W. (1958). *Through Paediatrics to Psycho-Analysis*. New York: International Universities Press.

Winnicott, D. W. (1960). The theory of the parent–infant relationship. In *The Maturational Processes and the Facilitating Environment*. New York: International Universities Press, 1965 (pp. 33–55).

Winnicott, D. W. (1962). The aims of psycho-analytical treatment. In *The Maturational Processes and the Facilitating Environment*. New York: Basic Books, 1965 (pp. 166–170).

Winnicott, D. W. (1965). *The Maturational Processes and the Facilitating Environment*. New York: Basic Books.

Winnicott, D. W. (1971a). The place where we live. In *Playing and Reality*. New York: Basic Books (pp. 104–110).

Winnicott, D. W. (1971b). Playing: A theoretical statement. In *Playing and Reality*. New York: Basic Books (pp. 38–52).

Winnicott, D. W. (1971c). *Therapeutic Consultations in Child Psychiatry*. New York: Basic Books.

Winnicott, D. W. (1971d). *Playing and Reality*. New York: Basic Books.

Winnicott, D. W. (1974). Fear of breakdown. In *Explorations in Psychoanalysis* (C. Winnicott, R. Shepherd and M. Davis, eds). Cambridge, MA: Harvard University Press, 1989 (pp. 87–95).

Index

acting in 164
acting out 103, 164
addictive love: bonds of 64–5, 68, 75;
central role in internal world 55;
diminution of 71
aggression: in Fairbairn's endopsychic
structure 63, 71
aggressive instinct 139
aliveness: and deadness 31–2, 33, 87
alpha-elements 46, 101, 102
alpha function 46, 102, 107, 158
ambivalence: of depressive position 80;
Freud's view of 29, 31; and mania 31;
and melancholia 7, 8, 18, 25, 29, 31;
between unconscious internal
objects 33
analyst: as-transference-mother 80
analytic frame: as medium for analyst's
hatred 81–2;
analytic relationship 41, 74–5, 79, 90,
115, 157, 160, 161, 166, 168,
169, 172
analytic style 117, 128; Bion's 118–37
analytic technique 83–4; 117
analytic theory: of alpha function 158;
Bion's 4, 35, 101, 102, 103, 158, 174,
176, 177; and clinical observation
157–8; of conscious and unconscious
experience 177; of depression 79;
Fairbairn's 55, 56–62; Freud's 12–13,
17, 22, 25; of instincts 144; Isaacs' 34,

35, 39, 51, 54; Klein's 19; of
melancholia 22; of narcissism 22;
object relations 11– 33; 51, 55–75,
144; of Oedipus complex 139–40;
Searles' 169; of transformations 102;
and truth 176; of unconscious
internal objects 25; way of not
thinking, use as 117, 127; Winnicott's
45, 77, 79, 90
ancestors: analytic 117, 141; becoming
147; creation of 142, 146; to
succeeding generations 141
animism 7
atonement: anterior to incest 152; of
oedipal relations 149–51, 152; and
Oedipus complex 156; of parricide
149–51, 152, 155, 156; and superego
149, 150, 153; in transmutation 150
Attention and interpretation 97, 98,
103–9, 118

bad objects: allegiance to 25; better
than no objects 59; love for 59
Balint, M. 56
Barros, E.&Barros, E. 44
"basic endopsychic situation" 60, 71
Bellow, S. 50
beta-elements 101, 102, 107
binocular vision 58
Bion, W.R.: alpha-elements 46, 101,
102; alpha function 46, 102, 107,

186

191